'The Protestant missionary mov...
Carey'. This oft-repeated gli...
misleading. And yet it is true that...
witnessed the amazing mushrooming of worldwide
mission with the tremendous growth of national churches
in every continent. But Ron Davies' book reminds us of
five earlier Christian leaders (Jan Comenius, Richard Baxter,
Cotton Mather, Jonathan Edwards, Count Zinzendorf).
He treats us to brief biographical backgrounds and then
proceeds to show their passion for international cross-
cultural mission. Some were personally involved in the
actual practice of mission overseas, others stimulated
missionary prayer and laid the theological and biblical
foundations for the later flowering of worldwide mission.
Each of the five also had a significant influence on Carey.
May this book be used of God to move today's church
to a greater self-sacrifice for the spread of the good news
of Jesus Christ worldwide - also with their particular
interest in the conversion of Jews and Muslims!

MARTIN GOLDSMITH
AUTHOR AND FORMER OMF
MISSIONARY IN ASIA

As a long-time admirer of Ron Davies's encyclopaedic
knowledge of the work of Jonathan Edwards, even I
was surprised to discover that the AD 2000 movement
owes its vision to the great New Englander. But there it is
in this remarkably revealing book. Writing in 1747,
Edwards reckoned it would be at least AD 2,000 before
the Christian faith would be globally accepted. Just one
item from this treasure-chest of information and insights
gleaned from the amazing characters Davies paints in a

readable, colourful style. How little we know them, but how much we owe them. For those who like to probe beneath the surface of missionary myths – read this fascinating book and be enriched, challenged and inspired.

CHRIS WRIGHT
LANGHAM PARTNERSHIP INTERNATIONAL
FORMER PRINCIPAL, ALL NATIONS
CHRISTIAN COLLEGE.

A Heart for Mission

Five Pioneer Thinkers

Ron Davies

Christian Focus

ISBN 1-85792-233-6

© Copyright Ron Davies 2002

Published in 2002
by
Christian Focus Publications, Ltd.
Geanies House, Fearn, Tain,
Ross-shire, IV20 1TW, Great Britain.

www.christianfocus.com

Printed and bound by
Omnia, Bishopbriggs, Glasgow

Cover Design by Alister MacInnes

Contents

Introduction

The Protestant Reformation began in the early part of the sixteenth century. The year 1517, when Martin Luther nailed his ninety-five theses to the door of the church in Wittenberg, is usually taken as the time when that great movement of spiritual renewal began. But Protestant **missionary work** did not begin in any significant way until nearly three hundred years later! It was not until 1792 when the English Baptist William Carey wrote his *Enquiry into the Use of Means for the Conversion of the Heathen,* that the Baptist Missionary Society was formed and the Protestant missionary effort really got under way.

What were Protestants doing for all this time? The answer is: many things, some of them legitimate but others less so, like arguing among themselves, making hair-splitting theological distinctions and excommunicating those who disagreed with them! And for most of this time Roman Catholic groups like the Franciscans, Dominicans and Jesuits were getting on with the work of missions.

There were, however, some exceptions among Protestants. For example, John Eliot and the Mayhew family were evangelizing the North American Indians in the seventeenth century, and men such as David Brainerd were doing the same in the middle of the eighteenth century. Chaplains accompanying the Dutch armies who drove the Portuguese out of Ceylon and

Indonesia in the seventeenth century substituted the Reformed faith for Roman Catholicism and in some cases did real missionary work among the local peoples. In 1706 German Pietist missionaries began work in the Danish colony of Tranquebar in India.

However, compared to the Roman Catholic missionary effort going on, and in the light of the vast numbers of people in the world without any knowledge of Christ, this was precious little.

In our final chapter we shall look at the one shining exception to the prevailing inactivity among Protestants – the Moravians.

It is also true that a certain amount of missionary thinking, planning and writing was going on, which in due course had a positive effect. Of course, thinking, planning and writing are no substitute for action, but they are often the necessary preparation for it, and when action does eventually take place it is more effective when it has been thought out than when it is completely unplanned.

The Christian leaders we shall be looking at in this book were **pioneer missionary thinkers**, but they were also men of action deeply involved in the work of the Gospel in their own situations, and also men with **a heart for mission**, as we shall see. Their influence in various ways prepared for the Protestant missionary explosion which began at the end of the eighteenth century and which carried on into the nineteenth and twentieth centuries and right up to the present. There is much for us to learn from them. As we shall see, their different contributions have a very modern ring to them.

In this book, we will be studying the thoughts and actions of men who, like John the Baptist, were 'preparing the way' for the modern Protestant missionary movement which, in the last two centuries, has circled the globe. Indeed, at the present time there is a missionary explosion from many of the countries which have been traditionally thought of as 'receiving countries'. There are reckoned to be between 8,000 and 10,000 Korean missionaries scattered throughout the world and their numbers are constantly increasing. Brazilian, Nigerian and Indian missionaries also are going out in increasing numbers to work in their own countries and continents, as well as further afield. How did it all start? What foundations were laid? What is the inner dynamic in Protestantism that has caused this amazing growth and which has been sustained for so long in spite of various 'ups and downs' spiritually and theologically and in many other ways? But why did it take so long to get going?

As we have said, the Protestant Reformation began in the sixteenth century and spread across northern and western Europe as well as considerable parts of eastern and central Europe. Northern Germany, Switzerland, the Netherlands, France, Britain, Scandinavia, Hungary, the Czech lands and Poland were all profoundly influenced, and strong Protestant Churches were established in all these countries, although the Catholic Counter-Reformation headed by the Jesuits later clawed back much of Poland, France and the Czech lands to Papal obedience. In the sixteenth century also, the Anabaptist movement spread from Switzerland to much of Europe, although excesses on the part of the militant wing, together with an intolerance from the mainline Churches, Catholic and Protestant, provoked sustained persecution which diminished their numbers and drove them into a ghetto kind of mentality out of which they have only begun to re-emerge in the latter part of the twentieth century.

The first generation of Reformers, such as Martin Luther, Martin Bucer and John Calvin, were certainly not parochially minded. They were strongly convinced of the sovereignty of God over the whole world and of His purpose that the Kingdom of Christ should be acknowledged by all peoples. They believed in the power of the Word of God to convict and convert the hearts of even the most degraded and hardened human beings, and they committed their lives to spreading that Word. Martin Bucer, in particular, believed on the basis of Romans 11:25 – 27, that through the preaching of the Word, the Jewish People would also come to faith in Jesus as their Messiah before the end of the age.

One piece of evidence which is often ignored when looking at the Reformers' attitude to mission is the public prayers they composed for use in the Churches. For example, in Martin Luther's 'German Mass and Order of Service' written in 1526, we read: '*After the sermon shall follow a public paraphrase of the Lord's Prayer*', which includes the words:

> That God our Father in heaven may look with mercy on us His needy children on earth and grant us grace so that His holy Name be hallowed by us and all the world ... That His Kingdom may come and be enlarged; that all transgressors, the sin-darkened, and

those in the bonds of Satan's kingdom be brought to a knowledge of the true faith in Jesus Christ, His Son, and the number of Christians increased.

Similarly Martin Bucer's 'Strassburg Liturgy' of 1539 has the following prayer:

We pray thee moreover for those who do not yet apprehend thy holy Gospel, but remain in error and depravity. Enlighten their eyes that they may also recognize thee as their God and Creator, and be converted to thy will.

And also:

Merciful God and gracious Father, we beseech thee further for all mankind. As it is thy will to be known as a Saviour to all the world, draw to thy Son, our Lord Jesus Christ, those who are still estranged from Him.

John Calvin develops this further in his 'Form of Church Prayers' for the Churches in Geneva (1542) and Strassburg (1545). The *Prayer at the end of the sermon* has the words

We pray thee now, O most gracious and merciful Father, for all men everywhere. As it is thy will to be acknowledged the Saviour of the whole world, through the redemption wrought by thy Son Jesus Christ, grant that those who are still estranged from the knowledge of Him, being in the darkness and captivity of error and ignorance, may be brought by the illumination of thy Holy Spirit and the preaching of thy Gospel to the straight way of salvation, which is to know thee, the only true God, and Jesus Christ whom thou hast sent... In such wise mayest thou be King and Ruler over all the earth, guiding thy people by the sceptre of thy Word and the power of thy Spirit, confounding thine enemies by the might of thy truth and righteousness. And thus may every power and principality which stands against thy glory be destroyed and abolished day by day, till the fulfillment of thy kingdom be manifest, when thou shalt appear in judgment.

They certainly prayed for the conversion of the world outside Christendom, but they did not actively work for it. Why? Firstly, they had more than enough to do with reforming the Church in Europe and establishing Biblically-based congregations. Apart from the task of recovering the Biblical gospel from the medieval overlay of Catholicism, they were also trying to clean up popular religion at the local level, which was a mixture of paganism and corrupt Christian beliefs and practices. Actually, in Geneva Calvin trained hundreds of pastors for reforming the Church in France and establishing new congregations there. France, together with the whole of Catholic Europe, was a 'mission field' as far as he was concerned.

Furthermore, the Swiss cantons as well as the Saxon dukedoms where the Protestant leaders worked were landlocked, with no access to the seas and oceans, and surrounded by hostile Catholic territories. In the sixteenth century the Protestant princes had no overseas colonies (such as the Catholic rulers of Spain and Portugal did) where the Catholic orders worked.

It has been pointed out that by abolishing the monastic orders, the Protestant leaders 'shot themselves in the foot' as far as missions were concerned. The orders, especially the Franciscans and Dominicans were the main missionaries in medieval Catholicism. The Jesuits, who developed out of the Counter-Reformation, were similar to them in their celibacy and in other respects. The Reformers, by their reinstatement of the value of marriage for Christian leaders and the importance of family life, deprived themselves of the means for missionary work which were still available to the Catholic Church.

Another instance of self-inflicted restrictions came from the Reformers' views on church offices and the relevance of the Great Commission. Calvin believed that, in the list of church offices mentioned in Ephesians 4:11, 'Apostles, prophets, evangelists, pastors and teachers', only pastors and teachers were permanent in the Church; the others were temporary and had disappeared at the close of the first century. Thus the task of pastors and teachers was to care for already established churches, not to found new ones. This was reinforced by their idea that the Great Commission only really applied to the original Apostles. It was not the permanent task of the Church of all times. This view became more pronounced in the next generation of Protestant leaders, but it was already held by a number of the first generation.[1]

They were certainly not impressed with the missions conducted by the Catholic orders, both the older ones like the Franciscans and Dominicans and the newer ones, such as the Jesuits. In fact, while some Jesuits like Francis Xavier went as missionaries to Asia, those in Europe were guilty of hunting down Protestants and forcing them to conform to Catholicism.

Martin Luther was initially favourably disposed towards the Jews and wrote about the need to evangelize them. However, he had a negative experience with some Jews he met and to whom he tried to speak about Jesus as their Messiah, and thereafter he became much more negative towards them! Both he and Calvin saw Muslims as enemies of the Gospel rather than people to be evangelized. They were influenced, as were many Catholics of the period, by the threat of the invasion of Europe by the Muslim armies of the Ottoman Empire.

It is sometimes pointed out that the Lutheran king of Finland did try to evangelize the Lapps who were within his domain but this was just an example of the widely held idea that a ruler had the duty to bring all his subjects to religious conformity. In the case of Calvin, he did support a missionary expedition to Brazil, although it went tragically wrong and came to nothing.

When all the evidence has been considered, it is still true that the first generation of Reformers did not have foreign missions at the top of their agenda. It remained for the leaders of the next two centuries to raise the profile of missions. We shall be looking at them later.

In choosing the five missionary thinkers who are the subjects of the following chapters we are not suggesting that they were the only ones in the Protestant churches to be concerned for the worldwide mission of the church. There were others who had a similar 'heart for mission' but whose views were largely ignored or rejected by their contemporaries. At this point it is worth mentioning another five who suffered this neglect or rejection.

In 1590 a Dutchman **Adrianus Saravia** (1531 - 1613), from 1582 to 1587 a preacher and professor in Leyden, published a treatise entitled *De diversis ministrorum evangelii gradibus, sicut a Domino fuerunt instituti*, which contained a chapter dealing with missions, showing that the Great Commission applied to the Church of all times. Theodore Beza, John Calvin's successor in the church at Geneva, wrote a strong refutation of the idea, arguing that the commission had been given to the Twelve Apostles alone and that they had fulfilled it. Calvin himself did not take Beza's line but it became very influential in the Reformed churches for the next several generations. One place where this was not the case was in Saravia's home country of the Netherlands where theologians like Justus Heurnius (1587-1651), Gisbertius Voetius (1589-1676) and Johannes Hoornbeeck (1617-1666) wrote complete theologies of mission. However there was no real response to the appeal from the Dutch churches and the Dutch East India Company which managed Dutch interests in the Asian colonies was more concerned with material profit than with spiritual matters.

In 1663 and 1664 an Austrian-born nobleman **Justinian von Weltz** (1621-c.1668) whose family fled to Germany because of persecution, produced a number of tracts in which he tried to stir up missionary interest among Lutherans. He proposed the setting up of a 'Society of the Lovers of Jesus'. Among other motives for world mission, he appealed to Matthew 28 and sought to show its relevance not only to the Apostles but to the Church of all ages. His appeals were rejected by Lutheran theologians who argued that, firstly, the command to go into all the world was a *personale privilegium* of the Apostles, like the gift of miracles, and they had fulfilled it; secondly, that the light of nature means that no man can be excused through ignorance; in addition, through Adam, Noah and the Apostles the Gospel had been preached throughout the world; and thirdly, it is the duty of the state to promote the true religion in all its territories through building churches and schools, and by appointing preachers. Disappointed with the negative response to his ideas, Justinian moved to the Netherlands, and from there sailed as a freelance missionary to Surinam, the Dutch colony in South America, where he died in obscurity.

A Church of Scotland minister of the eighteenth century who advocated missionary work was **Robert Millar** (1672-1752) of Paisley. His *History of the Propagation of Christianity and Overthrow of Paganism* was published in 1723 and provides a remarkably complete and balanced account of the history of Christian missions from the Apostolic era right up to Millar's time of writing. His final chapter concludes with 'a few arguments to excite us to act with holy zeal and concern in promoting the conversion of the heathen'. Among these he cites various Old Testament promises including Psalm 72:7-12, Isaiah 49:6, Isaiah 54:1-4 (from which William Carey later preached his famous sermon on the words 'Lengthen thy cords and strengthen thy stakes' with the two main points: 'Expect great things from God; Attempt great things for God'), and Psalm 2:8. He then argues that though these promises and many others like them have already been fulfilled from the Day of Pentecost up till his own time, 'yet there is a fuller performance of them to be expected before the end of the world' because of Jesus' prophecy in Matthew 24:14 that 'This Gospel of the Kingdom shall be preached in all the world for a witness unto all nations, and then shall the end come'. Millar comments:

> Tho' this was in part fulfilled by the propagation of the Gospel by the Apostles and Evangelists over the Roman Empire, before the end of the Jewish state... yet I see no reason why it may not be extended to a further propagation of the Gospel to the remote Heathens in Asia, Africa and America, before the end of time.

Indeed, says Millar, as there is to be a greater and more glorious conversion of the Gentiles in the future after, or at the same time as, the conversion of Israel (Rom 11:25), every Christian should pray, long for and work to promote such a great work. He then goes on to cite Matthew 28:19-20 to make the point that:

This duty of converting the nations, of instructing the ignorant, reclaiming the wandering, and bringing home the strangers to be members of the mystical body of Christ, is in a special manner incumbent upon the Pastors of Christ's Church. We are obliged to propagate the saving knowledge of Christ among all men so far as we can, and as orderly called by the very words of that commission from which we derive our office...

And this is not something for private individuals to take upon themselves; rather:

It may be the work of the gravest Convocations of the Clergy, of Presbyteries, Synods, or national Assemblies, regularly to send proper persons to labour in this work of *converting the nations*, to encourage them, and to notice their success; which would be of greater importance than most affairs that come under our consideration[!]

Millar's appeals did not meet with any real positive response and in fact it was not until 1824, a century later, that the General Assembly to which Millar appealed in the words above finally established a Committee for Foreign Missions to bring forward proposals for a Church mission to India.

In England in 1741, the Independent minister **Philip Doddridge** (1702-1751) proposed to two meetings of ministers, first in Norfolk and then in Northampton-shire, certain means for the advancement of Christ's kingdom, and in the following year he published them in connection with the printed edition of the sermon he had preached on both occasions. In 1741 he had become a 'Corresponding Member' of the Moravian 'Society for the Furtherance of the Gospel', although his interest in Moravian missionary work had actually begun in 1737, and in 1740 he had initiated a correspondence with Count Zinzendorf.

His suggestions were as follows:

> That pious people unite as members of a society; that they daily offer up some earnest prayer for the propagation the gospel in the world, especially among the heathen nations; that they attend four times a year for solemn prayer; that some time be then spent in reviewing the promises relating to the establishment of the Redeemer's kingdom in the world; that any important information of the progress of the gospel from foreign lands be communicated at these quarterly meetings; that each member contribute something towards supporting the expense of sending missionaries abroad, printing Bibles and other useful books in foreign languages; establishing schools for the instruction of the ignorant, and the like.

He tried to set up such a society in his own church in Northampton, where he also established a 'dissenting academy' to give the kind of education from which Nonconformists were excluded and to train men for the pastoral ministry. He had a long-standing interest in missionary work among the North American Indians, and when Jonathan Edwards' edition of David Brainerd's Journal was published in 1749, Doddridge was further fired up by it. He hoped that two of his students would go out to New York State to a school for Indian children but the students' parents prevented them. Doddridge says in his diary:

> Such is the weakness of their faith and love. I hope I can truly say that, if God would put it into the heart of my only son to go under this character [of a missionary] I could willingly part with him, though I were to see him no more. What are views of a family and name, when compared with a regard for extending my Redeemer's Kingdom, and gaining souls to Christ?

Within a few months of writing these words Doddridge died at the age of forty-nine. Among the Independent churches there was no response to his plans and ideas for another generation.

Thomas Coke (1747-1814) was an Anglican curate who joined the Methodists in 1777. He became one of John Wesley's chief lieutenants and was a key figure in much of Methodist life in Britain and North America. Among his many interests and activities, pride of place must be given to his concern for overseas missions but in this he met continual frustration and difficulty, often from unexpected sources as we shall see.

At the Methodist Conference of 1778 Coke advocated a Methodist mission to Africa following a request from two African princes who had been sold into slavery, but were later released and had returned to their home land. A legacy of £500 was available to cover the expense of the mission and two candidates had already expressed their willingness to go, but just before the Conference John Wesley wrote to one of them saying, 'You have nothing to do at present in Africa. Convert the heathen in Scotland.'[2] At the Conference Wesley decided that 'the call seems doubtful' and the plan was shelved. As John Vickers says (See the bibliography at the end of this book), 'It is not hard to imagine his [i.e. Coke's] disappointment as he listened to the discussion and witnessed the decision not to go ahead with the mission.'

Six years later, Coke tried again and published *A Plan of the Society for the Establishment of Missions among the Heathens* and tried to send missionaries to the East Indies. He prefaced it with an address to 'all the real lovers of mankind' and sent copies to many of his more well-to-do acquaintances. Anyone who subscribed two guineas was deemed to be a member of the society and when the *Plan* was published early in 1784 a total of £66.3 shillings had already been subscribed. However, he had not consulted John Wesley about it and when it came up at Conference in 1784, Wesley dismissed the idea suggesting that there was 'no call thither yet, no invitation, no providential opening of any kind'. In fact he had other plans to use Coke's talents and time. He was already eighty-one and foresaw various problems arising after his death, including the lack of a centre of union among the people called Methodists. Coke's legal contacts made him the ideal person to draft a *Deed of Declaration* which ensured the continuance of polity and the guarantee of property rights after Wesley's death. So Coke's energies were diverted in this direction. Wesley was also concerned about the state of Methodism in the newly independent United States of America after the War of Independence. Francis Asbury (1745-1816) a Methodist preacher born in the Midlands, who had sailed to America in 1771 as Wesley's 'General Assistant' for that country, was the only English-born Methodist preacher who had stayed in America during the war.

There was the need for ordained men who could baptize and administer the Sacrament of the Lord's Supper. Wesley set apart Coke as 'Superintendent' of American Methodism and instructed him to ordain Asbury. Coke duly set out for the United States in September 1784 (the first of nine visits), ordained Asbury, who was then elected as fellow superintendent (which title was soon changed to 'Bishop'). Over the years he travelled widely in the thirteen states of the Atlantic seaboard[3] and played a significant part in the organization of American Methodism, although, because he divided his time between Britain and America (and the West Indies as we shall see), he was never fully accepted by Asbury or the American Methodists.

By 1786 Coke was ready to try again! He had learnt from his previous failures and this time obtained Wesley's commendation before making his proposal and also was less ambitious in the areas of the world he sought to reach. He published his *Address to the Pious and Benevolent. Proposing an Annual Subscription for the Support of the Missionaries in the Highlands and Adjacent Islands of Scotland, the Isles of Jersey, Guernsey and Newfoundland, the West Indies, and the Provinces of Nova Scotia and Quebec* in time for the 1786 Conference. Wesley and the preachers endorsed Coke's proposals but left the responsibility of implementing them completely to him. This meant that he had single-handedly to raise the money, recruit the missionaries and seek to educate the societies to support the work – on top of his other work of preaching, writing, overseeing the Irish work of the Methodists, sorting out legal matters and travelling overseas! The financial burden meant that he spent most of his own money and that of his first and second wives when he married in later life. He also was constantly begging for money, sometimes from house to house, to support those whom he had recruited.

His first attempt to sail to Nova Scotia with potential missionaries to establish the work there was frustrated as a gale blew the ship seriously off course and they finished up in Antigua in the West Indies! However, he saw the providence of God in this and establishing missions in the various islands of the area became a dominant passion of his life. From 1792 onwards he was able to send missionaries to most islands in the West Indies as well as Sierra Leone, Nova Scotia, Ireland, France, Gibraltar and the Cape. Not all of these were successful; in 1795 an attempted mission to the Fula people of West Africa failed dismally. This was due, at least in part, to Coke's over-optimistic views of the candidates who volunteered for the mission, who in the event were unable to cope. On the other hand, he had increasingly to get volunteers from outside the ranks of those already in the itinerant ministry in England as Wesley and his successors were unwilling to lose talent from the work at home.

The Conference of 1790, the last to be attended by Wesley himself, appointed a committee 'for the management of our affairs in the West Indies' but again it was left to Coke to organize. In 1793, the Conference authorized a 'general collection' to be taken in each society for the West Indian work, which was running up a sizeable debt, but again Coke was given the task of implementing it. The financial problems of the mission continued in the following years and came to a head in 1803 when Coke was on the last of his visits to the United States. A Committee of Finance and Advice was set up, which was a mixed blessing as Coke had to spend considerable time liaising with the committee in addition to writing a six-volume commentary on the Bible, preaching and frantically begging for money for the mission.

In 1813, after years of impassioned appeals from Coke, the Conference finally authorized a mission to Asia. Coke himself headed a group of six missionaries who set out in December of that year. He died en route to India in May 1814 and was buried at sea in the Indian Ocean; the rest of the party continued and began the work without him.

The Wesleyan Methodist Missionary society was finally established in 1818. The century that followed saw the full fruition of the pioneer efforts so painfully begun by Thomas Coke.

Further note on John Wesley's attitude to world mission

The question which probably arises in many minds after reading the above account of Thomas Coke's frustrations is: Why did John Wesley, the man who 'look[ed] upon the whole world as [his] parish' act in the way he did towards Coke's suggestions? After all, in 1705 his father Samuel Wesley had presented a comprehensive plan to Queen Anne for the evangelization of the East, offering to go himself as a missionary to Abyssinia, India or China! In 1712 his mother Susannah came across an account of the Pietist missionaries from Halle who had gone out to India in 1706, was 'greatly affected' by it and communicated her interest to her husband and her children.

In 1735 John and Charles sailed for Georgia as SPG missionaries to the Indians, although they both returned disillusioned, Charles in 1736 and John in 1738. In one of his worst moments he characterized the Indians he met as 'gluttons, drunkards, thieves, dissemblers, liars'. He acknowledged later that he had gone out to America more to save his own soul than to save the Indians.

One of Wesley's published sermons was on 'The General Spread of the Gospel' (1783) where he showed his belief in world mission, but it seems that concern with matters at home made him feel that the time was not right. Could it also be that 'the whole world as my parish' concept included the idea that he had to be in control of the mission in any part of his world parish and ideally he had to think of it first? Certainly, he tried to keep his hand firmly on the North American branch of Methodism even after the Revolutionary War, although Francis Asbury and others politely but firmly refused such attempts.

The Reformers, Puritans and other Protestants of the previous centuries are often accused of being uninterested in world mission because of their Calvinism. Perhaps we can learn from Wesley that not every refusal to move out to the world is theologically motivated. There may be other reasons, which we may find more or less acceptable. We should probably be slow to judge those in former generations who accomplished so much for the Kingdom of God.

Notes:

[1] See 'The Great Commission from Calvin to Carey' in *Evangel* 14/1 (Summer 1996) pp 44-49. In addition there are two books which give useful background information: Timothy George, *Faithful Witness: The Life and Mission of William Carey* (IVP, 1991) (this has Carey's *Enquiry* in full in an Appendix) and Michael A G Haykin, *One Heart and One Soul: John Sutcliff of Olney, his friends and his times* (Evangelical Press 1994).

[2] Wesley seems to have been echoing the words which a Methodist leader had written three years earlier in a letter about John Prickard the other volunteer, who was obviously committed to missionary work, 'John Prickard wants to go to mission work to America among the American Indians. He's needed here. Indians! Why go to America to look for them! Their black souls are visible at home.'

[3] On his first visit Asbury introduced him to his new 'circuit' by sending him on a nine-hundred-mile horseback tour of American Methodism!

1

JAN AMOS COMENIUS
(1592 – 1670)

Education and Mission

The year 1992 was remembered by the British Royal Family as an *annus horribilis*. It was also a year which saw a number of important anniversaries, most notably that of Columbus' discovery of America in 1492. It was also the two hundredth anniversary of William Carey's *Enquiry* mentioned above, which was followed by the formation of the Baptist Missionary Society and numerous other societies, and which launched the 'Great Century of Missions'.

An anniversary that was widely celebrated in many places, but sadly not in Britain, was the four hundredth anniversary of the birth of Jan Amos Comenius. In his home country of Czechoslovakia (which itself passed into history at the end of 1992), celebrations took place throughout 1992, and in a total of seventy other lands some public recognition was given to the life and work of Comenius. In Britain, however, there was no recognition of the fact; indeed it seems that there was complete ignorance of the man and his work. Europe, either past or present, does not seem to concern Britons very much!

Comenius is mainly remembered in his own land as an educational innovator. He was a pioneer of more humane methods of teaching children than were customary at the time. He also set forth revolutionary ideas for the teaching of languages, and, most importantly from our point of view, he argued for the use of education as a missionary method. Indeed, his vision for missionary work was well ahead of his time, as were his ecumenical ideas and his educational methods.

Who was this man of whom English-speaking Christians today are so woefully ignorant?

Birth and early life

Jan Komensky (Comenius is a Latinized form) was born in eastern Moravia on 28 March 1592. He was orphaned when he was about twelve years old. This was the first of many tragedies in his life but his indomitable God-centred confidence and optimism through his life of tragedy and exile, together with his pastoral and national concerns, his educational and ecumenical writings and endeavours, are a monument to the triumphant power of faith, hope and love over difficulty, disappointment and adversity.

He went to Herborn and Heidelberg in southern Germany for his theological training and when he returned in 1616 he became a school teacher in the school where he himself had studied and was also ordained as a minister in the *Unity of Brethren*, a 'Protestant' Church which had existed in the Czech lands since 1457, sixty years before the start of the Protestant Reformation! (See the extended note at the end of this chapter for more on the background of the *Unity of Brethren*.) In 1618 he became a pastor in Fulneck, in Moravia, where he married.

In hiding
In 1620 the Czech Protestant armies were defeated by the combined Catholic armies at the Battle of the White Mountain near Prague, the first decisive battle in the Thirty Years War (1618 – 1648) between Protestant and Catholic states in Europe. A number of the Protestant leaders were publicly executed in Prague, Catholicism was brutally imposed on the total population of Bohemia and Moravia and all the Protestant nobility and clergy were expelled from the land. Comenius, together with a number of other ministers, went into hiding, and in the same year, while he was still absent from home, his wife and two children died in a plague. His personal tragedy and the sufferings of the church, together with his faith, are evident in his writings at that time: *The Man of Sorrows* and *The Name of the Lord is an Impregnable Fortress*. While in hiding he also composed what became, and remains, a popular devotional classic in the Czech language, *The Labyrinth of the World and the Paradise of the Heart*. His Christ-centred devotion and also his ecumenical concerns are apparent in this work which in many ways prefigures John Bunyan's *Pilgrim's Progress* which was written fifty-five years later.

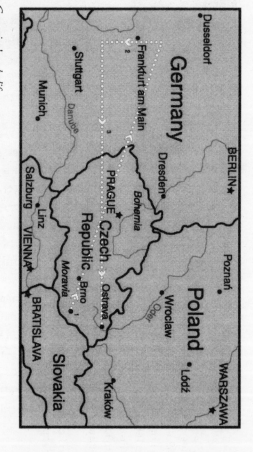

Comenius' early life

1. Born & brought up (inc. early education) in Eastern Moravia. 1592-1611

2. Further education in Herborn & Heidelberg. 1611-1614

3. Returns to Moravia as school teacher & then pastor. 1614-1628

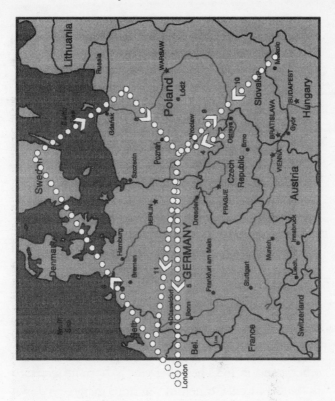

Comenius' later life – the years of exile

4. Beginning of exile in Leszno, Poland. 1628-1641

5. Visit to London. 1641

6. Sweden. 1642

7. Elbing, Prussia. 1642-1648

8. Return to Leszno. 1648-1650

9. To Sarospatak, Hungary. 1650-1654

10. Back to Leszno. 1654-1656

11. Final years in Amsterdam. 1656-1670

31

Exile in Poland

In 1624 he remarried, and four years later, led a band of exiles across the mountains into southern Poland. It had been decided that the Brethren from Moravia (the eastern part of the present-day Czech Republic) should seek refuge in Slovakia, and the Bohemians (from the western part of the country) in Poland. Comenius, although a Moravian, decided to go with the Bohemian Brethren.

At Leszno he helped the refugees to settle in their new home (in the hope that they would eventually be able to return to Moravia when the war was over). He pastored them conscientiously but also involved himself in a vast number of other enterprises. He arranged for the Brethren's printing press to be secretly brought from Kralice in Moravia, and began to write and publish his works on educational reform, especially on language teaching, together with other works including *The Labyrinth*. He also began to try out his own methods in schools and, in 1632, he was elected bishop and secretary of the Brethren! Comenius was not a man to sit down and lament his problems!

Visit to England

In 1641 Comenius visited England in the hope of gaining support for one of his more idealistic schemes, an encyclopaedic 'pansophic' college. This would embrace all knowledge, including scientific and biblical, and would teach the peoples of all nations the truth which would bring an end to war and discord! His optimism knew no bounds although we may feel he was rather naive in his expectations! The programme as he envisaged it would start with Christian nations and go from there to Muslims, pagans, and finally the Jews who, as the apostle Paul hoped in his *Letter to the Romans*, would come to faith in Christ through jealousy, when they saw the Gentiles enjoying God's blessings. As he says in *The Way of Light:*

> The result of that light which is promised is the conversion of all peoples to the Church, so that Jehovah shall be King over all the earth.... Then the Gospel of the kingdom shall be preached in the whole circle of the world, for a witness to all the peoples, before the end shall come.... Then the earth shall be filled with the knowledge of God as the sea is covered with waters.... And then there will be universal peace over the whole world; hatred and causes of hatred will be done away, and all dissention between men. For there will be no ground for dissenting, when all men have the same Truths clearly presented to their eyes.

And he closes the book with the following paraphrase of the Lord's Prayer:

> Our Father who art in heaven, may Thy name be hallowed in the whole world! Let Thy Kingdom come even now to the whole world! May Thy will be done even now in the whole earth as it is in whole Heaven! Through the whole of Europe, of Asia, of Africa, of America, through the Magellanes [the southern parts of present-day Chile and Argentina], and through all the islands of the sea, may Thy Kingdom come, may Thy will be done!.... Raise up men to write Thy purpose in books, but books such as Thou

Thyself mayest write in the hearts of men; make
schools to be opened in all parts of the world to nurse
Thy children! And do Thou raise up Thine own school
in the hearts of all men in the whole world that they
may ally themselves together for Thy praise; be Thou
Thyself leader of the choir of Thine elect.

Whatever we may think about the viability of
Comenius' hopes there is no doubt about his worldwide
vision and missionary zeal.

Sweden and Prussia

Soon after Comenius arrived in England the Civil War
broke out. No-one was interested in his educational and
missionary ideas, being preoccupied with the conflict
between King and Parliament and their respective
armies. According to Cotton Mather, in his *Magnalia
Christi Americana,* either at this time or later, Comenius
received an invitation to emigrate to Puritan New
England, possibly with a view to becoming president
of the newly founded Harvard College there. Comenius
himself speaks in one of his writings of the group of
English friends who invited him to England having in
mind to present to him 'a plan for the propagation of
the Gospel among the heathen', which may refer to an
invitation to New England both to Harvard and as a
missionary to the Indians.

He also received two other invitations, one from the
Roman Catholic Cardinal Richelieu to come to Paris,
and the other from a Belgian industrialist, Louis de Geer,
to go to Sweden. Probably because he still had hopes
of the Brethren being allowed to return to their

homeland and wanted to be at hand in case this happened, he accepted the Swedish invitation, and on the way, visited Rene Descartes the Catholic philosopher, who had shown an interest in his plans for a 'pansophic' college. After interviews with the queen of Sweden and the Swedish chancellor, he eventually agreed to spend time reforming the Swedish school system, and in November 1642 moved his family to Elbing in Prussia (now Elblag in present-day Poland) as a convenient point between Sweden and Leszno in southern Poland.

In a very non-ecumenical age Comenius had an extraordinarily large circle of acquaintances from all branches of the Church as well as moving in royal circles!

Return to Leszno

He remained in Elbing until he completed his educational reforms in 1648. He returned to Leszno in August 1648, having been elected Senior Bishop of the Unity. Two tragedies struck in the same year. His second wife died soon after they arrived back in Poland and, shortly after, he heard the bitter news that the Peace of Westphalia, which ended the Thirty Years' War between the Protestant and Catholic nations, made no provisions for Protestants in Bohemia and Moravia. They lived under the rule of the Catholic Habsburgs and were given no permission to practise their Protestant faith. He complained bitterly to the Swedish chancellor, who had promised to support the Unity of Brethren's case in return for Comenius' educational reform work, but he was rebuffed. He felt betrayed, both personally and on behalf of the Church, but he continued to encourage them from the pulpit and in print.

In 1649 he published a *History of the Community of the Czech Brethren,* and in 1650 he wrote his *Bequest of the Dying Mother, the Unity of Brethren,* in which, with the death of his second wife still in his mind, he portrayed the Unity as a mother calling her children around her on her death-bed to divide her legacies among them. He felt that there was no future for the Unity of Brethren as a separate denomination if they were not allowed to return to their own country and worship according to their own conscience, and so he urged members of the Unity to join the Protestant church where they found themselves. At the same time, he felt that all other Churches were deficient in many aspects of faith and practice compared with the Unity of Brethren.

In words that have only been fulfilled in our own time, he addressed his own people:

> Nor can I forget thee, thou Czech and Moravian nation, my native land, now that I take my final leave! ... I trust God that after the passing of the storm of wrath which our sins have brought upon our heads, the rule of thine affairs shall again be restored to thee, O Czech people!

Not until 1918 when Czechoslovakia became an independent nation as the Habsburg Empire was broken up, did the Czech people gain the right to rule themselves, and then only for twenty years. For another half-century, from 1938 until 1989, the country was first under Nazi and then under Soviet control. Only with the 'Velvet Revolution' of 1989 and the collapse of the Soviet Empire did Comenius' words become true – a long time to wait!

Hungary

In 1650 a general synod of the Unity of Brethren was called in Leszno to decide what to do in the light of the situation in Bohemia and Moravia. In spite of Comenius' words in the 'Bequest', they decided not to disband, but to brave whatever the future had in store for them. As for the final result, they were determined to 'leave it to our chief pastor, Christ'. Comenius was chosen to visit the Brethren in Slovakia, to communicate the decisions to them. (Slovakia was part of Hungary, which was also under the Habsburgs, but was outside of the bounds of the 'Holy Roman Empire' and did not suffer the same religious intolerance as Bohemia and Moravia.)

He visited the congregations in Slovakia, and went on from there to Sarospatak in northern Hungary where the Hungarian Prince Sigismund Rakoczy had his palace. He had written to Comenius expressing interest in his educational ideas and inviting him to visit.

On the way, Comenius met a former school-fellow, Nicholas Drabik, a minister of the Unity, who claimed to possess the gift of prophecy. He told Comenius that God had designated Sigismund as future king of Hungary, and that Sigismund would liberate the whole of Europe from papal power, including his beloved Moravia and Bohemia, and would also make it possible for the gospel to be preached to the Turks. Comenius was at first inclined to doubt the truth of what Drabik was prophesying because he had already had experience of the failure of his supposed oracles, but he was eventually convinced otherwise. Subsequent events showed that he would have been better advized to continue his scepticism.

Comenius moved his family to Sarospatak (he had married a third time in 1649) and stayed there until 1655, when he returned to Leszno. Some of his educational reforms were accepted, although not without opposition, but his grand plans for a 'pansophic' university were not taken up. Nor was there any indication of Sigismund fulfilling Drabik's prophecies about the liberation of Europe from papal power. He died prematurely in 1654. Drabik then transferred the prophecies to Prince George Rakoczky, but he also died without fulfilling them!

Comenius was desperate at the plight of his flock and so appealed through an English friend to Oliver Cromwell to help the suffering members of the Unity in their exile. Cromwell offered them land in Ireland where they could settle, but Comenius turned down the offer and the contacts came to an end. In the light of events in our own day, one wonders what effects it might have had on subsequent history if the offer had been accepted!

Tragedy in Leszno

Comenius returned to Poland, feeling that the Hungarian episode had been a failure. His sufferings and disappointments were, however, not yet ended. In 1655 Charles X of Sweden had invaded Poland and had achieved a number of initial successes against John

Casimir, the Polish king, who was a strong Catholic.
The lord of Leszno was among a number of Polish
leaders who had welcomed the Swedish king and
Comenius wrote a pamphlet in praise of Charles, which
was published by the Leszno city authorities.

In 1656, however, the tide of battle turned against
Charles and the Polish Catholics decided to punish
Leszno for supporting the Swedes. On 29 April it was
looted and burned to the ground by Polish Catholic
soldiers. Comenius and the Brethren lost everything they
possessed; they literally had only the clothes they wore.
Comenius lost his savings, his unpublished manuscripts,
including a Latin-Czech dictionary on which he had
worked for forty-six years, and his 'pansophic' writings,
some of which were almost ready for publication. The
Brethren lost their two official libraries and their printing
press. The disaster was complete.

Final years in Amsterdam

Comenius appealed to various countries for funds to
help the homeless refugees, who eventually settled in
Upper Silesia, Hungary, Lusatia and Brandenburg.
Comenius himself accepted refuge in Amsterdam,
where he spent the last fourteen years of his life. In
spite of all the disappointments and sufferings of his
life, including the crowning tragedy of Leszno, he still
continued writing and publishing! He reprinted many
of his own works that had been destroyed, together
with a number of prophecies which Drabik and others
had given about events in Europe. Many of these had
to do with the restoration of Czech independence and

the restoration of the Brethren's fortunes. Sadly, they were not fulfilled, at least not in Comenius' lifetime.

His missionary zeal was undimmed and in Amsterdam he planned a translation of the Bible into Turkish, to prepare the way for Muslim evangelism. Comenius entrusted the actual translation to someone else but had general oversight of the project and wrote a preface addressed to the Turkish Sultan urging him to read the Scripture as he ruled over many Christians. As with so many of his projects, it came to nothing, but not for want of trying! He died in November 1670 in Amsterdam and was buried in Naarden. An exile for much of his life, he also died in exile.

Lessons for today

What lessons are there for us to learn from Comenius' life? Certainly, he is a stirring example of Christian perseverance. In spite of personal tragedies, disappointed hopes, frustrated plans, the failure of much of his life's work, he never gave up and he never became bitter. Some of his ideas were too grandiose, at least in the confused situation in Europe in the seventeenth century.

Whatever view we take of the possibilities of genuine predictive prophecy beyond the pages of the Bible, Comenius' acceptance of the claimed oracles was probably because what was 'prophesied' was what he wanted to hear, especially regarding the restoration of the fortunes of the Czech nation and Church. It should stand as a warning to us.

His ideas on education, at least those on how children learn, have influenced teaching methods in Central

Europe and Russia for many generations, even though his large-scale plans did not come to fruition.

Education as a missionary method has had mixed results over the past two hundred years of Protestant missionary work. Where large amounts of money and missionary resources have been put into education, the outcome has often been people who are well-educated but still unconverted and in recent decades missions have moved away from such work. However, the desire for education remains high in the Two-Thirds world and missionaries still have a part to play in this.

Extended note on the Unity of Brethren (Latin: Unitas Fratrum)
The *Unitas Fratrum* has its roots in the reforming activity of Jan Hus, the Czech preacher who was martyred in 1415. Hus was a contemporary of John Wycliffe who was seeking similar changes to the life of the Roman Catholic Church in England. His fiery preaching in the Bethlehem Chapel in Prague, together with his writings which called for reform, and the public anger provoked by his death, produced a popular movement of revolution and later the 'reformation before the reformation' in Bohemia in which a latent missionary element is present. In fact even before Hus himself we can see elements of the same thing in his predecessors.

One of these reforming predecessors in Prague, Jan Milic of Kromeriz (died 1374)[1], was strongly eschatological in his preaching, but with a strong ethical and practical bent also. In his *De Antichristo* as well as in his preaching (for which, unusually, instead of Latin he used Czech – with a strong regional accent!), he castigated the anti-Christian elements which he saw in society and the Church. He stopped short of declaring either emperor or Pope to be the Antichrist, but he did criticize them both by name. In 1365 he proposed to Pope Urban V that he should launch a vast missionary campaign to reach the whole of the known Christian world, so that pagans and Jews, seeing a truly penitent church, would themselves be converted! The New Jerusalem of Revelation 21-22 fascinated him, not merely as the object of hope, but as something to be realized here and now, albeit imperfectly. He sponsored the building of a hospice for reclaimed prostitutes in the centre of the 'red light' district in Prague, naming it 'New Jerusalem'. He also began a preachers' college in the same area, naming it 'Nazareth', and after his death, the 'Bethlehem Chapel' was founded by his friends, where Jan Hus and others preached the gospel in the Czech language.

A modern Czech theologian, Amadeo Molnar, sees in the emphasis of Milic, Hus and others, the germ of a missionary faith which was later developed by others, and which we may see as a further element in the religious background of the later Moravians. He observes:

> The eschatological intention of the founders of the Bethlehem Chapel is clearly evident: the Word of God is not bound, they proclaimed; it must spread freely in the language of the people and so prepare the way for the realization of the divine promises. Here, underlying, is the germ of a thought which I should describe as missionary. It is included in the conviction that Christian people should renew their faith through

listening to the Word. The reform of the Church itself must be undertaken with a view to the future conversion of the whole of humanity. The mission was to be realized not so much by an active expansion of institutionalized Christianity as by a reducing and concentrating movement of the eschatological remnant which the minority Church of Christ crucified really is.[2]

A further development of this idea is seen in the 'Four Articles of Prague', which became the watchwords of the Hussite Revolution. Probably drawn up by one of Hus' colleagues, Jacoubek of Stribo ('Little James', referring to his stature!) they, interestingly, anticipate the later Reformation emphasis on the 'marks of the true Church'[3]. They call for reform of the Church in the following ways:

That the Word of God be preached everywhere, and through all Christendom, which is not being done.... That the Holy Sacrament of the Body and Blood of God, in both kinds, bread and wine, be freely given to all true Christians who are not barred from it by deadly sin; just as our Saviour inaugurated and ordered it.... That priests and monks should be deprived of great earthly possessions and unlawful power and should live exemplary lives and be led back to the ways of Christ and the Apostles.... That all mortal sins, especially of a public nature should be properly prohibited and punished, including those committed by nobles, monks, priests, etc....

The emphasis on discipline in the third and fourth articles was to be a hallmark of the later Unity of

Brethren after 1457 when they had separated from the national Church to form what was essentially a 'gathered church' of believers. As we shall see when we look at Zinzendorf and the Moravians who sprang from the *Unitas Fratrum*, the move away from the territorial idea, or *Landeskirke* concept, was an essential step in 'freeing up' the Church for worldwide mission.

In the Hussite movement in Bohemia, that move was made through the influence of a farmer and amateur theologian, Peter Chelcicky. In Prague the Hussite archbishop, John Rokycana, preached fiery sermons denouncing sin in the nation, its leaders and its people, but the national church structure made it difficult, if not impossible, to implement reforms or to apply the kind of discipline called for in the 'Four Articles of Prague'. The archbishop's nephew, Rikor (or Gregory) and some of his friends, who wanted such a reform, were sent by Rokycana to consult Chelcicky. His advice led them to form the Unity of Brethren in 1457. Interestingly, Chelcicky himself did not join them, but his writings continued to influence them in their ideas and practice. His *Net of Faith* (1521) is an attack on the corruption introduced by the Constantinian settlement in the fourth century and a call for a return to the purity of the pre-Constantinian Church. He devotes page after page to a description of the missionary dynamism of the first believers. They were men and women who had 'died to the world' in Christ, and so were able to have an interest in the salvation of the whole world through Christ. This salvation, which manifests the greatness of God's love for all mankind, is great enough to save several worlds at once, not only this one! To quote Molnar again:

> The missionary influence of the Church is conditioned, according to Chelcicky, by the refusal to use methods which are disapproved of in Jesus' Sermon on the Mount.... In order to conquer the world again, the Church must pluck up courage to lay down its traditional weapons.... The way of the Christian mission is that of a minority Church not retreating before martyrdom.

These ideas became an essential element in the thinking of the Unity, which was exemplified in their sufferings over the next two centuries, and continued to influence the Renewed Unity as it was reborn in Herrnhut in the 1720s (See Chapter 5 – Count Zinzendorf).

Notes:

[1] Milic himself built on the reforming preaching of Conrad of Waldhausen, an Augustinian canon taken from Vienna to Prague by the Holy Roman Emperor Charles V, a Bohemian. It is a sad fact that the great majority of these names and the facts surrounding them are almost completely unknown to English-speaking Christians.

[2] Amadeo Molnar, 'The Czech Reformation and Missions' in *History's Lessons for Tomorrow's Mission* Geneva 1960, p. 129.

[3] Martin Luther and John Calvin believed that the 'marks of a true church' were the preaching of the pure gospel and the right administration of the sacraments. Martin Bucer added a third: the exercise of church discipline. These three came to be the accepted norm in much of Protestant Christianity.

2

RICHARD BAXTER
(1615 – 1691)

Evangelism and Mission

The name of Richard Baxter is probably more well-known than that of Comenius, at least to English-speaking Christians. Baxter was a Puritan minister during one of the most unstable periods of English history which saw civil war, the execution of the king, a period of republican government, the re-establishment of the monarchy and the persecution of non-conforming ministers and Christians.

He was largely self-educated; he never enjoyed good health; he spent time in prison during the reign of James II, and like many other Puritan pastors was excluded from preaching for many years. Nevertheless he had a very active preaching ministry for at least twenty years, produced hundreds of writings, large and small, was involved in political and ecclesiastical activity and was a zealous advocate of missionary work. His vast literary output included three major folios of theology, as well as scores of practical and controversial writings, ranging from a few pages to a classic devotional work of eight hundred pages! His 'Practical Works' alone, which are still in print, fill four heavy volumes of small print.

Birth, conversion and early life

He was born on 12 November 1615 near Shrewsbury and spent the first ten years of his life in his grandfather's home because of his mother's poor health. However, he moved back home at the age of ten and was deeply impressed by his parents' faith in Christ, which compared very favourably with the local vicar and his assistants, whom Baxter described as 'ne'er-do-wells' and one of whom was 'the excellentest stage-player in all the country, a good gamester and a good fellow'!

During his first six years' schooling he had four different teachers, two of whom were ignorant, according to Baxter. At the free school in Wroxeter he began more advanced studies and read a number of Puritan writings including those of William Perkins and Richard Sibbes. Of Sibbes' *Broken Reed* he says, 'He opened more the love of God to me, and gave me a livelier apprehension of the Mystery of Redemption and how much I was beholden to Jesus Christ.' At Wroxeter he also studied under a godly minister, Francis Garbett, reading logic and other subjects, but also being concerned over his lack of 'a lively apprehension of things spiritual'. However, he found peace in 'a hearty love of the Word of God, and of the servants of God'. During this time he met two Separatists, Joseph Symonds and Walter Craddock, who helped him spiritually but did not influence him with their Separatism. After a few months in London, where he was repelled by court life, he returned home on his mother's death in 1634, spent four years in private study and was ordained to the Anglican ministry at the age of twenty-three.

He first taught at a free grammar school in Dudley, Worcestershire, was then assistant minister in Bridgnorth, Shropshire, until in 1641 he became minister of the church in Kidderminster, again back in Worcestershire. (All of these moves, apart from the time in London, were all in a radius of about forty miles.) During this time he became increasingly drawn away from a belief in episcopacy, as he saw it in the Anglican Church, to a form of Presbyterianism.

Preaching and writing

His move to Kidderminster in 1641 was soon followed by the outbreak of the Civil War the following year. Baxter preached for a few days to the Parliamentary army near Edgehill before the first battle of the Civil War there in 1642, and became an army chaplain at Coventry for the next three years until he was appointed as chaplain to Whalley's regiment in the New Model Army in 1645. In 1647 he retired from the army because of a serious illness and during his recuperation in the home of Sir Thomas Rous, he wrote the first part of his *Saints' Everlasting Rest*, an eight-hundred-page classic on heaven and the way in which Christians should think about and be prepared for it. He felt at the time that he looked death full in the face but at the same time experienced 'the sufficient grace of God'.

He returned to Kidderminster in 1647 and remained until 1661. His ministry there was the most fruitful Puritan pastorate anywhere recorded, resulting in the conversion of nearly the whole town. In fact it is probably right to speak of the time of his ministry there as one of revival, although he faced all kinds of opposition to his work.

When he first arrived the majority of the people were ignorant and crude but he was encouraged by the existence of a few spiritual believers. His preaching of the Gospel to the unconverted was marked by urgency, fervency and concern for his hearers; in his often-quoted words, he 'preached as a dying man to dying men'. His public prayers also impressed his hearers with his own intimacy of fellowship with God, 'his soul took wing for heaven and rapt up the souls of others with him'. He was wholehearted and conscientious in all of his pastoral work; 'Preach I must, I must visit the sick, instruct the ignorant, resolve the doubting, comfort the dejected and disquieted soul, admonish the scandalous and relapsed. As far as I am able these must be done and very much more.'

He faced a considerable amount of opposition to his work, including attempts to blacken his character. On one occasion he was falsely accused of consorting with a prostitute, but his accuser later admitted that he had seen Baxter on horseback sheltering from a thunderstorm under one side of a large hedge and the lady of doubtful reputation on the other side, each unaware of the other's presence! He was verbally abused in church more than once; he was physically attacked and once narrowly escaped being murdered.

His health was never good but he persevered in his work, speaking of 'my pains, though daily and almost continual did not very much disable me from my duty; but I could study and preach and walk almost as if I had been free.'

Under Cromwell's church settlement, which established Independency, Baxter formed the interdenominational Worcestershire Association of Pastors pledged to practise congregational evangelism and to maintain church discipline. In addition to regular preaching in Kidderminster and further afield, he had regular home meetings for his fellow ministers and for members of the congregation. He and his assistant systematically visited every family in Kidderminster to 'catechize' them. To quote an account written shortly after his death:

> He preached twice every Lord's day before the civil war; afterwards once; and once every Thursday, besides occasional sermons in the lectures at Worcester, Shrewsbury, Dudley, Sheffnall, etc. On the Thursday evenings such as were so disposed met at his house, one of them repeated the sermon, and afterwards they propounded to Mr Baxter any doubts they had about it, or any other case of conscience, which he resolved. On Mondays and Tuesdays in the afternoon, in every week, he and his assistant took fourteen families between them for private catechizing and conference, spending about an hour with a family. Every first Wednesday in the month he had a meeting for parish discipline. Every first Thursday in the month there was a meeting of the neighbouring ministers for discipline, and amicable disputation about matters theological.

His *Reformed Pastor* (1656), which has been reprinted many times and is still in print today, enshrines many of the insights gained from his Kidderminster experience, which he shared with the Worcestershire ministers.[1]

In 1658 he wrote his *Call to the Unconverted* (1658), an 'electrifying pioneer evangelistic pocket-book that sold by tens of thousands', in the words of Dr Jim Packer.

With the Restoration of the monarchy in 1660, Baxter moved the following year to London, where he preached and lectured to large crowds who came to hear him. Spies from the Royalists who were now back in power attended his sermons to try to trap him, but on one occasion he preached on 'Making Light of Christ' with such force that the agents left the church in a hurry!

He also attended the Savoy Conference, which was a largely abortive attempt to reconcile the varying ecclesiastical viewpoints, Anglican, Presbyterian and Independent. Baxter wrote a *Reformed Liturgy* and presented it to the conference but it was rejected and the following year (1662) the Act of Uniformity resulted in those Puritan ministers like Baxter who could not accept the full Restoration Settlement of Anglicanism leaving their public ministries.

In the same year Baxter surprized both friends and enemies by marrying a lady twenty-one years his junior. When she died in 1681 he wrote a work expressing his love for her and his estimate of her worth, *Breviate of the Life of Mrs Margaret Baxter*. He was imprisoned for a week in 1669, but spent the next few years concentrating on writing. He lived in various places in and around London.

Later life

After ten years of silence he resumed his public preaching, but was constantly harassed and persecuted by bishops and magistrates for breaching the various laws that had been enacted after the Restoration to silence the Puritan preachers. When James II came to the throne in 1685, things got much worse for him. He was charged with attacking episcopacy in his *Paraphrase of the New Testament* and was eventually hauled before the notorious and brutal Judge Jeffreys, who was consumed by hatred for all Puritans, especially Baxter. Although Baxter was now seventy, Jeffreys raged at him as 'an old rogue who poisoned the world with his Kidderminster doctrine' and charging him with seditious behaviour. He further attacked him as 'a conceited, stubborn, fanatical dog – that did not conform when he might have been preferred; hang him!' He was fined and might have been whipped through the streets had not pressure been brought on the bishop of London and others. Baxter spent twenty-one months in jail.

He lived to see the Glorious Revolution of 1689 when James II fled (and Jeffreys was imprisoned in the Tower of London where he died) and the establishment of a Protestant succession with William and Mary. He died in physical pain but peace of heart on 8 December 1691.

Baxter wrote voluminously and often without sufficient care. His large output included evangelistic, devotional, pastoral, doctrinal and controversial works. Regarding controversy he said in later life, 'In my youth I was quickly past my fundamentals and was running up into a multitude of controversies; but the older I grew the smaller stress I laid upon these. And now it is the fundamental doctrines of the catechism which I highest value.'[2] He also said, 'Controversies I have written of, but only to end them, not to make them' and it is to Baxter we are indebted for popularizing the maxim, 'In essentials unity; in non-essentials liberty; in all things charity.'

Missionary interest and involvement

Baxter's evangelistic and pastoral gifts and interests were seen in his ministry in Kidderminster as well as in his writings. However, he also had a strong concern for the salvation of all mankind which showed itself in a variety of ways, including prayer, lobbying, action, and writing letters, tracts and pamphlets. In one of his writings published after his death he says: 'No part of my prayers are so deeply serious as that for the conversion of the infidel and ungodly world.' In 1661 as we have seen, he composed a *Reformed Liturgy*, which he presented to the Savoy Conference of bishops and ministers, in which several of the prayers are for the conversion of Jews, Muslims and all non-Christians. For example, in *The General Prayer* the minister is to pray:

> Let all the earth subject themselves to thee, their King. Let the kingdoms of the world become the kingdoms of the Lord, and of his Christ. Let the atheists, idolaters, Mahomatans, Jews, and other infidels, and ungodly people, be converted. Send forth meet labourers into the harvest, and let the gospel be preached throughout all the world. Preserve and bless them in thy work.

The 'New England Company' was set up in the Commonwealth period to support and publicize the missionary work among the North American Indians that John Eliot and others were doing. Baxter supported it from the time it was set up and, after the restoration of the monarchy in 1660, lobbied and used every way possible to secure the renewal of the company's legal status which was rescinded by Charles II. Because of his part in the Civil War (having been a chaplain in the Parliamentary Army for a time), he had to work behind the scenes, but he was eventually successful in his efforts and the 'New England Company' was reconstituted. (In fact, the Company continues to exist till the present time, although the work it supported has long ceased.)

His contacts with John Eliot

John Eliot was an English Puritan pastor who, in 1631, joined the 'Great Migration' from England to New England. The following year he was appointed pastor of a church in Roxbury in Massachusetts Bay. Over the next several years he taught himself the language of the local 'Indians' (or native Americans) and in 1646 began to preach to them on a regular basis. He formed the converted Indians into a number of communities or 'praying villages' and cared for their spiritual and material needs. He translated the whole Bible into their language together with books, catechisms and a hymn book.

Baxter admired John Eliot in his missionary work and did all he could to support the work. He also maintained a correspondence with him for nearly thirty-five years (until the time of Eliot's death a year before his own), and was constantly encouraging him in his work. In one of his first letters Baxter says, 'I know no work in all the world that I think more highly and honourably of than yours; and consequently no person whom I more honour for his work's sake.' He met much discouragement in trying to raise support for Eliot's work but he persevered.

When Eliot wrote that his work as pastor of a White congregation limited the time he could spend in Indian evangelism, Baxter encouraged him to go full-time as a missionary (advice which Eliot did not take!). He says, 'Were I your neighbour, and did believe that forsaking your Church would enable you to do much more service to the poor Indians than your church service cometh to, I should cast in my judgment that it were your duty so to do, and to be only the Apostle to the Indians.'

In 1670 Baxter wrote to his New England friend: 'The industry of the Jesuits and friars and their successors in Congo, China and Japan shame us all, save you.' And after Eliot's death, he wrote to Increase Mather: 'I knew much of Mr Eliot's Opinions, by many Letters which I had from him. There was no Man on Earth, whom I honour'd above him. It is his Evangelical [i.e. missionary] Work, that is the Apostolical Succession that I plead for.'

In his letters to Eliot, and also in many published writings, he argued for the idea that the Great Commission of Matthew 28:18-20 still applied to the church today. This seems obvious to us, but from the time of the Reformation in the sixteenth century until William Carey at the end of the eighteenth century, the idea was not generally accepted among Protestants.

Baxter was an exception to the general rule and argued the case with forcefulness. He also argued for a special class of 'unfixed (i.e. itinerant) ministers', in other words evangelists and missionaries, who could devote all their time to this work. It was at least another hundred years before his ideas were really taken up.

Other missionary interests

In addition to his interest in missions to the American Indians, he also encouraged one of his wealthy friends to finance the translation into Arabic of a work on apologetics by a Dutch writer, and then wrote to the Dutch East India Company suggesting that the book be spread by agents of the Company 'to the end Christianity may be established among those infidels'.

In many of his writings he expounded the task of the ministry of the gospel as he saw it. The preaching of the gospel is the great means ordained by God that men should be converted. The first duty of the gospel ministry is to make the world Christian and gather men into the church by teaching and baptizing them.

He even suggested that a 'College for Conversion' should be set up which would prepare missionaries to go to all nations, including the Jews, because 'The most eminent work of charity is the promoting of the conversion of the heathen and infidel parts of the world'. Heathen, Mohammedans, and Jews need to be converted, but the behaviour of Christians is often a stumbling-block. The latter two groups have access to some truth in their religion, but they still need the preaching of the gospel. Baxter's millennial views did not have a place for a national conversion of the Jews, but he did long for their salvation, and, in fact, urged his more millennially minded contemporaries: 'Do not only pray for them, but study what is in the reach of your power to do for their conversion.'

Lessons for today

Richard Baxter is an example of a person who lacked many educational advantages, suffered ill health for much of his life, was prevented by circumstances from doing all he wanted to do as a Christian, experienced opposition and persecution for much of his ministry but who, nevertheless, achieved a tremendous amount in his life, and since his death, by his writings. He was a man with a consuming desire for the salvation of others, both those in his own sphere of influence and others further away. He lived in the firm belief of the reality of the eternal world and this made him busy to serve God and his fellow human beings in this one. If we feel that we lack the gifts and opportunities which others may have, if we suffer from ill health, if we feel that our situation limits our usefulness for God, we may take encouragement from Richard Baxter. Similarly Baxter gives the lie to the idea that a Christian who has a strong sense of spiritual realities is 'so heavenly minded that they are no earthly good!' Baxter had a greater sense than most of heaven and its reality. He was of great earthly usefulness.

Notes:
[1] The full title was *Gildas Salvianus: The Reformed Pastor, showing the nature of the Pastoral work; especially in Private Instruction and Catechizing; with an open CONFESSION of our too open SINS:*

Prepared for a Day of Humiliation kept at Worcester, December 4, 1655, by the Ministers of that County, who subscribed the Agreement for Catechizing and Personal Instruction at their entrance upon that work, By their unworthy fellow Servant, Richard Baxter, Teacher of the Church at Kederminster. (!)

[2] The Westminster Shorter Catechism (1648).

3

COTTON MATHER
(1663 – 1728)

Ecumenism and Mission

Cotton Mather – another name that very few people today have heard of! Who was he and what relevance does he have to missions?

In fact, although most British Christians may not have heard of Cotton Mather, scholarly American church historians undoubtedly have: indeed, he is a favourite target of scorn, anger and even hatred for many of them! One writer has described him as the 'ugly toad of Colonial New England' because of the way in which he seems to attract such criticism! Mather serves as the target for everything about American Puritan Christianity of the seventeenth century that modern writers hate! Perry Miller is an example. He says that Mather 'in a hundred respects [was] the most intransigent and impervious mind of his period, not to say the most nauseous human being...' although he also has to admit that in other respects he was 'the most sensitive and perceptive, the clearest and most resolute'. The part he played in the notorious Salem Witchcraft Trials in 1692 has been used to blacken his name in American schools for generations. One writer in the middle of the nineteenth century said: 'The present generation of youth is taught that nineteen persons were hanged, and one was pressed to death, to gratify the vanity, ambition, and stolid credulity of Mr Cotton Mather.' As we shall see, this is a travesty of the truth. A twentieth-century American writer, recording the ill treatment Mather received as a student at Harvard, rejoices that 'that insufferable young prig Cotton Mather was being kicked about, as he so richly deserved'. So much for scholarly impartiality!

Cotton Mather certainly had his bad points (don't we all!). But he hardly deserves the bad press he has received in the twentieth century from scholars. In fact, with the well-known American penchant for going to law, if Cotton Mather came back today he could start a large number of multi-million dollar lawsuits which he would have a very good chance of winning!

His life and ministry

Cotton Mather (1663-1728) was a minister in Boston, New England who came from a family of ministers. His grandfather, Richard Mather (1596-1669) had emigrated from England, along with many other Puritan pastors, as also did John Cotton (1584-1652), whose widow Sarah married Richard Mather in August 1656. Richard had four sons by his first wife Katherine who had died the previous year, all of whom became ministers. The youngest of these, Increase Mather (1639-1723) also married twice. His first wife was his step-sister, Marie Cotton, one of John Cotton's children! She bore him six children, the first being Cotton Mather, named after his maternal grandfather – hence the name which is rather strange to modern ears (although his father's name sounds even stranger). Just to make things more complicated, Increase's second wife was the widow of another Rev. John Cotton, the grandson of **the** John Cotton who emigrated from England!

Cotton's father was a minister of the North Church in Boston from 1664 onwards and in 1674 was also made an overseer of Harvard College. He accumulated the finest and most extensive library in the whole of the American colonies and his son was introduced at a very early age to its riches. From an early age he also followed his father in his devotion to Christ and genuine, practical godliness. His relationship with his father, whom he also joined in later life as co-minister of the North Church, was close and affectionate. He says that he accounted among his chief blessings 'the Life and Health of my dear Father, whom I may reckon among the richest of my Enjoyments'. As one writer commented, 'Cotton Mather never observed any other law of God quite so faithfully as the Fifth Commandment.'

By the time he entered Harvard at the age of eleven, he had already read a number of the Greek and Latin classics, as well as the Greek New Testament, and had begun the study of Hebrew grammar. In his spiritual life by the age of fourteen he was already keeping whole days of prayer and fasting, and at sixteen joined the North Church as a communicant. However, as we have seen, he was not popular with some of his fellow students and was ill-treated by them. This may have accounted for his proneness to depression, his hypochondria and the stammer he developed.

The stammer was the reason for his deciding initially not to enter the pastoral ministry, even though he did preach occasionally. He began the study of medicine, continued at Harvard as a tutor and was awarded the M.A. degree in 1681. At the age of nineteen he was invited to become the pastor of a church in New Haven which John Davenport, another of the first generation of English ministers to go across the Atlantic in the 1630s, had planted. However, he chose to remain as his father's unordained assistant and to continue his studies. The Boston congregation called him to the pastorate in 1684 and in 1685 he was ordained and became his father's co-minister.

He continued and increased the vigorous pastoral programme which his father had begun in the neighbourhood of the North Church. This included evangelism among the poor and criminals and the creation of a religious society for young men in the south of the town. Increase, who had spent the years 1657-1661 in Britain, returned there in 1688 to try to gain a new royal charter for Massachusetts which would give more autonomy. He was away until 1692. Cotton continued his pastoral work during this time, in which there was an average of twenty-five new members added each year, apart from 1691, when there was a mini-revival and forty-nine were added.

He was a prolific author, beginning with some poems in the early 1680s and broadening out to include sermons, pamphlets and books. Four hundred and forty-four of his works were published during his lifetime and many more he produced remain in manuscript form, among them an enormous commentary on the

Bible, the *Biblia Americana*. He was also a great activist and 'do-gooder' (one of his works was *Bonifacius, or Essays in Doing Good* [1710], and in 1711 he began a practice of writing each day in his diary 'a GOOD DEVISED', abbreviated as 'G.D.'), setting up societies for various causes and writing letters to governors, magistrates and others to agitate for reform.

He was also a deeply spiritual man, who maintained a strict devotional life of prayer and fasting, regularly setting aside days for this. He regularly prayed for world-wide mission and also recommended the practice to others in many of his writings. His great hope and prayer was for a worldwide revival which would include a renewal of spiritual gifts. He believed that the prophecy of Joel 2:28-32 was still to be fulfilled in a far greater way than in the Early Church or up to the present time: 'That effusion of the Spirit by which the Primitive Church flourished might be as drops, which will be followed by Mighty Showers for the Accomplishment of this Prophecy still to be expected in the Latter Days.' In particular, the gift of tongues, communicated by angels (presumably based on his understanding of 1 Corinthians 13:1: 'If I speak in the tongues of men and angels') would be evident in the great revival preceding the Return of Christ.

In fact, he believed, contrary to normal Protestant understanding as seen in the Reformers and the Puritans (although similar to some of the German Pietists), that spiritual gifts were still available for Christians today. However, he warned against placing too much emphasis on them: 'A soul sanctified with the love of God, and of CHRIST, and of our neighbour, is altogether to be preferred before all the *Extraordinary Gifts* of the Holy Spirit.'

In his diary he records his various spiritual experiences, including angelic visitations and 'words from the Lord' which he believed he received from time to time. When he was twenty-three, he had a notable experience which he records in Latin. Translated, it reads:

A strange and memorable thing. After outpourings of prayer, with the utmost fervour and fasting, there appeared an Angel, whose face shone like the noonday sun. His features were those of a man, and beardless; his head was encircled by a splendid tiara; on his shoulders were wings; his garments were white and shining; his robe reached to his ankles; and about his loins was a belt not unlike the girdles of the peoples of the East. And this Angel said that he was sent by the Lord Jesus to bear a clear answer to the prayers of a certain youth, and to bear back his words in reply. Many things this Angel said which it is not fit to set down here. But among other things not to be forgotten he declared that the fate of this youth should be to find full expression for what in him was best: and this he said in the words of the prophet Ezekiel [quoting Ezekiel 31:3,4,5,7,9]. And in particular this Angel spoke of the influence his branches should have, and of the books this youth should write and publish, not only in America but in Europe. And he added certain special prophecies of the great works this youth should do for the church of Christ in the revolutions that are now in hand. Lord Jesus! What is the meaning of this marvel? From the wiles of the Devil I beseech thee, deliver and defend Thy most unworthy servant.

He records other angelic visitations in his diary and further believed that he had his own special angel.

As is clear from the citation he also believed in the possibility of Satanic deception as well as his activities and that of other evil spirits, especially in the matter of witchcraft. His book *The Wonders of the Invisible World* which he wrote in December 1692, the year of the Salem Witch Trials, gives other examples of demonic possession and activity over the previous thirty years in New England. When the apparent outbreak of witchcraft and Satanic activity occurred in Salem in May 1692, Cotton Mather's involvement was minimal. In fact, he was very ill during most of the four months from May till August when the whole affair was at its height and he was one of those who counselled caution in accepting hearsay evidence and showed pastoral concern to those who were involved. There is no evidence for the above-mentioned slanders that have been repeated so often.

Cotton Mather was a devoted family man; he married three times and had thirteen children, five of whom, including twins, died in infancy. His son Increase ('Cressy' as he was known to his father) was a cause of great grief to his parents, being an ungodly, immoral wastrel, who was drowned in 1724 at the age of twenty-five on a voyage from Bermuda to Newfoundland. One of his other sons, Samuel, became a minister and published a 'Life' of his father.

His interest in missions

One of the most interesting attitudes in Mather, and
the reason for his inclusion in this book, is his interest
in missions. There are at least three aspects to this
interest; firstly, as a missionary biographer as he writes
up the missionary activity of John Eliot and others in
seventeenth century New England; secondly, the work
he did to publicize the work and gain support for it
when he was appointed as one of the Indian
Commissioners; thirdly, his involvement with the work
being done by German Pietist missionaries in Asia and
his ideas for evangelical co-operation.

Missions to the Indians

The only work of Mather currently in print is his is
Magnalia Christi Americana, (published by the *Banner of
Truth Trust* as *The Great Works of Christ in America*). It is
a large, rambling, incompletely-digested collection of
various histories, accounts, lists, statements, poems and
other pieces of literature, all having to do with the
history of the Protestant churches in New England,
which Mather sees as a continuation of the work of
God described in the Bible. For Mather, as well as for
many of his contemporaries, the planting and growth
of the New England churches is to be seen as part of
the continuing saga of redemptive history, reproducing
in typological form the experience of the biblical people
of God.

Mather devotes considerable space in his book to
an account of the life and work of John Eliot (1604-
1690), whom we met in Chapter 2. Eliot was a Puritan
minister born in Hertfordshire, who emigrated to the

New World as part of the 'Great Migration' of 1630 and the following decade. He was pastor of an English congregation near Boston but also spent a considerable part of his time as a missionary to the Indians. He translated the whole Bible into their language, together with many books and tracts. He preached, baptized, and formed his converts into churches and also established special villages or 'praying towns' composed of the Indian Christians. Cotton Mather uses a letter his father, Increase Mather, had written a number of years before to a Dutch professor of Hebrew who had shown interest in Eliot's work among the Indians.

Mather also describes the missionary work of the Mayhew family on the islands of Martha's Vineyard and Nantucket off the coast of New England and he uses the examples of Eliot and others to urge that more missionary work should be done, not only among the North American Indians, but among Black slaves, the Welsh, the Irish, and many others. His proposals are worth quoting to show his genuine missionary concern.

Firstly, he says,

> May the People of New-England ... be encouraged still to prosecute, first the Civilizing, and then the Christianizing of the Barbarians, in their Neighbourhood; and may the New-Englanders ... make a Mission of the Gospel, unto the Mighty Nations of the Western Indians whom the French have been unsuccessful in converting and influencing.

The motives for doing this are 'Politick as well as Religious'; if the Indians are not civilized and

Christianized they may attack us and harm us, says Mather!

Secondly, he urges that the plantation owners in America and the West Indies who live off the labours of the Negro slaves should not 'deride, neglect and oppose' means of bringing them to the Lord. They are 'Reasonable Creatures', who are not merely to be used 'to serve the Lusts of Epicures, or the Gains of Mammonists'. Mather's concern for Negroes continued throughout his life. He was interested in their spiritual welfare as well as their physical wellbeing. He fell short of suggesting their actual emancipation, even though a friend of his, Judge Samuel Sewell, did so a year later. (Up until this time it had been early Quakers such as George Fox, George Keith and John Woolman who had advocated the abolition of slavery altogether.) In his diary, which was not intended for public view, he says:

> I have at my own single Expense for many years, maintained a Charity-Schole for the Instruction of Negroes in Reading and Religion. A Lieutenant of a Man of War, whom I am a Stranger to, designing to putt an Indignity upon me, has called his Negro-Slave by the Name of COTTON-MATHER.

Others, it seems, followed suit, 'that so they may ... assert Crimes as committed by one of that Name, which the Hearers take to be *Me*'!

Thirdly, he suggests that the English Nation has not done enough 'that the Welch may not be destroy'd for the lack of Knowledge', nor 'to reclaim the Irish, from the Popish Bigottries and Abominations, with which they have been intoxicated'. In Mather's day England and Scotland (with the exception of the Highlands and Islands) had more organized Protestant churches than either Wales or Ireland.

Fourthly, he makes the suggestion to the trading companies who were multiplying as different parts of the world opened up:

> May the several Factories and Companies, whose Concerns lie in Asia, Africa, or America, be persuaded ... that they are under a very particular Obligation to communicate of our Spiritual Things upon those Heathens by whose Carnal Things they are Enriched and may they therefore make it their Study, to employ some able and pious Ministers, for the instruction of those Infidels with whom they have to deal, and honourably support such Ministers in that Employment.

He is arguing here for the practice of chaplains of the trading companies being involved in evangelizing the native population. This had been done by the Dutch in Ceylon and Taiwan although Mather had already criticized the superficial nature of the enterprise. He appears to be in favour of the practice itself, but critical of the way it had been done by the Dutch.

In the fifth place, he urges that England should provide Bibles, Catechisms and Christian books for Eastern Orthodox Christians in the Greek, Armenian and Russian Churches, and elsewhere, where they have 'little Preaching and no Printing, and few Bibles or good Books', and that these should be 'scattered among them'.

'Who knows', he says, 'what Convulsions might be hastened upon the whole Mahometan World by such an extensive Charity!' Interestingly, while at first sight it might seem that this was one of the many impractical suggestions which Mather was in the habit of making, the Society for Promoting Christian Literature (S.P.C.K.) was formed in 1699, the year after Mather completed the *Magnalia*, with this purpose in mind.

Sixthly, he proposes the formation of 'well-composed Societies, by whose united Counsels, the Noble Design of Evangelizing the World, may be more effectually carried on'. He has in mind 'sufficient Numbers of great, wise, rich, learned and godly Men in the Three Kingdoms' of England, Scotland and Ireland, who should combine to form such societies on the analogy of 'some other Celebrated Societies heretofore formed from such small beginnings' which would soon grow and 'gather vast Contributions from all well-disposed People to Assist and Advance this Progress of Christianity'. The New England Company, of which his father Increase was, at the time of writing, a Commissioner, would provide the most obvious example to imitate, but Cotton Mather also had experience of religious societies in New England as well as knowledge of similar ones in England.

Some such societies as he envisages here were formed in the next few years after he penned these words; the Society in Scotland for Propagating Christian Knowledge (S.S.P.C.K), beginning in 1701 as a small "Society for the Reformation of Manners", and developing into an agency which sought to evangelize the Highlands and Islands of Scotland, and eventually sponsoring missionaries among the North American Indians; also the Society for the Propogation of the Gospel in Foreign Parts (1701), concerning the activities of whose missionaries Cotton Mather so often complained! However, the great age of Protestant missionary societies did not begin for nearly another century, and, when they did, even though they did not gain the support of the whole church, they were far more of a 'grassroots' phenomenon than that which seems to have been envisioned by Mather.

However, in order to show that his vision did include the actual sending of missionaries, he urges that:

> Lastly, May many Worthy Men ... get the Language of some Nations that are not yet brought home to God; and wait upon the Divine Providence, for God's leading them to, and owning them in their Apostolical Undertakings ... Let them see, whether while we at Home ... are Angling with Rods, which now and then catch one Soul for our Lord, they shall not be fishing with nets, which will bring in many thousands.

He concludes with the exhortation and encouragement:

> Let no man be discouraged by the Difficulties, which the Devil will be ready to clog such Attempts against his Kingdom with ... If Men had the Wisdom, To discern the Signs of the Times, they would be all Hands at Work, to spread the Name of our Jesus into all the Corners of the Earth. Grant it, O my God; Lord Jesus, Come quickly.

From this it can surely be said that Cotton Mather had a genuine missionary concern for the world of his day. Like Richard Baxter, he was ahead of his time.

Commissioner of Indian Affairs

In 1699 Mather was appointed as one of the New England commissioners of the London-based 'New England Company' which had been formed over fifty years before to support the work of Indian missions (see the previous chapter). Following the Indian War of 1675 when many Christian Indians were killed and much of Eliot's life-work was ruined, interest in the work of missions declined. Mather and his friend Samuel Sewell did all they could to revive interest. Mather wrote books, tracts, letters to influential people, as well as preaching sermons, in this effort. He also urged prayer for the conversion of the Jews to Christ. The result of all his effort was meagre but not for want of trying on his part.

The Pietist connection

Ten years after he became an Indian Commissioner he made contact with German Pietists who were involved in missionary work in India. This marked the full flowering of his own interest in missionary work as well as his own distinctive contribution.

Through a friend who was visiting England at the time, Mather was put in contact with Anthony William Boehm (1673-1722), a German preacher who arrived in London in 1701, opened a school, and later became assistant chaplain to Prince George of Denmark, the consort of Queen Anne.

Boehm had been trained in Halle, which was the centre of Pietism, the renewal movement in German Lutheranism. One of the key leaders of Pietism, August Herrman Francke, was a close friend of Boehm. Francke wrote a book about the work of Halle and Boehm translated it into English and got it published in London. In 1706 the first two missionaries went out from Halle to India and the next year a second edition of Francke's book referred to this. Mather began a correspondence with Boehm and Francke in 1709 and later with the missionaries themselves. His own knowledge and understanding of the wider purposes of God were strengthened by this correspondence but he also began to make his own distinctive contribution.

Mather, in fact, became part of an international network of news and ideas relating to mission. In 1709 or 1710, through Boehm's influence, the S.P.C.K. in London began to take notice of the mission in India, and in 1711 wrote to the missionaries inviting them to become correspondents of the society. At the same time the society supplied them with a printing press, and a gift of fifty pounds to help carry on the work. Thereafter, letters (in Latin) from Ziegenbalg and Plütschau, were sent from Tranquebar to London in ships of the East Indies Company, translated into English, read at the S.P.C.K. meetings, and published by Boehm; the originals were then sent on to Francke in Halle, who translated them into German for publication, with copies also being sent to Copenhagen for the information of the Danish Church. After a time Mather received his own copies of the correspondence and began contributing.

In one letter to Francke, the original of which still survives, he defends America against old European ideas that it was the 'outer darkness' spoken of in Matthew 25: 30! He gives a very positive picture of the work of missions among the North American Indians, and suggests that 'true and original Christianity' is to be found in New England.

He also introduces his ideas about 'the eternal gospel', an ecumenical basis of faith, which, he hoped, would unite all truly renewed Christian groups (such as Halle and New England), and would be preached to the whole of the heathen world. He summarizes the essence of the faith in a number of his writings, including a bilingual tract he wrote for the North American Indians. The 'Maxims of the Everlasting Gospel' as he refers to them are three in number:

> In the First Place; The One GOD, who subsisteth in Three Persons, the Father, and the Son, and the Holy Spirit; and who in the Beginning did Create the World; is to be Embraced and Adored for OUR GOD. It must be the Principal Aim of our Life, in all things to yield Obedience unto Him. And it must be our most hearty Care, to Avoid every Thing which His Light shining in our Soul shall condemn as an Evil Thing.
>
> In the next Place; The CHRIST, who is the Eternal SON of GOD Incarnate in our Blessed JESUS, is our only Redeemer; who Dying for us, has offered a most Acceptable Sacrifice to the Divine Justice, on which relying by Faith we become Reconciled unto God; and under the Conduct of Him who being received up into the Heavens, now Reigns on the Throne of GOD, we are to expect a wonderful and

unspeakable Blessedness for our Immortal Soul, whereto our Body shall be Re-united in a Glorious Resurrection, when he shall Return unto us to Judge the World.

Lastly; Being filled with the Love of GOD and of CHRIST, we must most Heartily Love our Neighbours; and for ever go by that Golden Rule, Whatsoever you would have Men do unto you, do you even the same unto them.

As an orthodox Congregational minister, Mather adhered strongly to the Savoy Declaration which was, in effect the same as the Westminster Confession of Faith, but in his genuine attempts to find a common basis on which to unite all believers, he put forward this brief summary which is Trinitarian, Christocentric and personal. It is interesting to note that in our own century the movement towards breaking down denominational divisions between Christian churches found its initial impulse among those involved in missionary activity.

Lessons for today

Mather's interests and activities were so many, as we have seen, that the lessons we can draw for today are also many! Mather's reputation since his death certainly warns us to expect that what others may think of us is not necessarily the truth! At times he certainly did invite criticism by his tendency to self-advertisement and we should beware of anything that smacks of this! He came from a fine Christian family and continued in the faith of his parents and grandparents although, sadly, his own favourite son did not. Many of Mather's schemes came to nothing and his missionary interests did not see immediate results. From these things also we may learn.

4

JONATHAN EDWARDS
(1703 – 1758)

Eschatology and Mission

Jonathan Edwards – another unlikely candidate for inclusion in a book on missionary thinkers! By many Christians he is remembered only as a 'hellfire' preacher, who in his famous (or infamous) sermon, 'Sinners in the Hands of an Angry God' portrayed unbelievers as held by God over hell like a spider over a fire, likely to fall into the flames at any moment.

This, of course, is a caricature both of Edwards and of his famous sermon. Like his contemporaries, John Wesley and George Whitefield, both of whom preached often on the danger of unbelievers going to hell, Edwards was a preacher with a consuming desire that men and women should come to Christ, enjoy his salvation and escape the awful reality of judgment. Like John the Baptist, he warned his contemporaries to 'flee from the wrath to come'.

For much of his active life Jonathan Edwards was a Congregational pastor in the town of Northampton, Massachusetts. The furthest he ever travelled was southwards to New York and eastwards to Boston. And yet his vision was unhindered by such geographical restraints, embracing the divine purposes for the world. Without exaggeration it is possible to speak of Jonathan Edwards as missionary theologian, missionary biographer, missionary trainer, missionary strategist, missionary administrator, missionary advocate – and missionary!

The basic facts of his life do not immediately make this clear, giving only hints of his deep missionary concerns. He was born on 5 October 1703, the fifth child and the only son, of the Rev. Timothy Edwards and his wife, who had a total of eleven children. He grew up in East Windsor, Connecticut, where his father was the minister, entered Yale College in 1716, graduated in 1720, and remained for another two years for advanced studies in theology. During that time he experienced 'a new sense of things', a new conviction of divine glory and excellence. After a brief ministry in New York, in a Presbyterian church, and a summer of study in East Windsor, he returned to Yale in 1723 to receive his M.A. degree. He was appointed a tutor in 1724, but severe illness prevented his fulfilling his duties for several months. In 1726 he accepted the invitation to join his ageing maternal grandfather Solomon Stoddard (1643-1729), of Northampton, Massachusetts as assistant pastor. In July 1727 he married Sarah Pierrepont, who bore him eleven children, eight daughters and three sons. During Edwards' ministry at Northampton, a local revival broke out in 1734 and 1735, and a more extensive awakening covering the whole of New England and beyond, in 1740-1742. Edwards wrote a number of his key works describing, analysing and defending the revival as a genuine work of God. Controversy with his congregation over a number of points in the late 1740s caused him to resign in 1750, and in 1751 he moved to Stockbridge, Massachusetts, a remote frontier settlement where he served as pastor of the church and missionary to the Indians. Controversy continued with some members of the church there, which was eventually resolved in Edwards' favour. He served as pastor and missionary administrator and continued to write. In 1757 he was invited to the College of New Jersey as President; he reluctantly agreed, but when on reaching Princeton, he was vaccinated against smallpox, he contracted the disease, and died on 22 March 1758.

It is only as we begin to fill out the details that we find the deep missionary vision and concern which undergirded much of his thinking, writing and acting. There is evidence of his concern for the spread of the gospel in the world at least from the beginnings of his preaching ministry. During his brief pastorate in New York when he was only nineteen, we read in his 'Personal Narrative':

> I had great longings for the advancement of Christ's kingdom in the world; and my secret prayer used to be, in large part, taken up in praying for it. If I heard the least hint of any thing that happened in any part of the world that appeared in some respect or other to have a favorable aspect on the interests of Christ's kingdom, my soul eagerly catched at it; and it would much animate and refresh me.

It was also the topic of many conversations he had with his friend John Smith, in whose mother's house he stayed during his time in New York and is reflected in at least one of the sermons he preached in New York. And it was something which stayed with him as he developed and matured. Writing nearly twenty years later, he describes his continued attitude:

> My heart has been much on the advancement of Christ's kingdom in the world. The histories of the past advancement of Christ's kingdom have been sweet to me. When I have read histories of past ages, the pleasantest thing in all my reading has been, to read of the kingdom of Christ being promoted.... And my mind has been much entertained and delighted with the scripture promises and prophecies, which relate to the future glorious advancement of Christ's kingdom on earth.

His missionary concern was deep-seated, permanent – and Christ-centred. It was a concern for the glory of Christ and the spread of his kingdom in the world.

He was twenty-four years old when he moved to the town of Northampton to become the assistant minister to his grandfather Solomon Stoddard. For many years Stoddard had been rather negative in his attitude to the North American Indians but in later years he wrote two books in which he argued that it was the duty of the White settlers to evangelize them. Edwards was strongly influenced by his grandfather and this would have strengthened his own views on evangelism and mission. The year he moved to Northampton he made a note in his 'Catalogue', where he recorded the books he wanted to read or buy a book on the history of missions mentioned in our introduction, *History of the Propagation of Christianity*. He eventually obtained his own copy in 1731, signed it, later loaned it to his father and eventually took it to Princeton with him when he became president of the College of New Jersey shortly before his death. (The fact that he took this book shows the value he placed on it as he was 'travelling light' when he rode to Princeton on horseback and only took the books he really needed and valued.)

In 1734, the year in which revival broke out in Northampton and the Connecticut valley, Edwards was involved in the establishment of a new missionary venture, the Stockbridge mission, where seventeen years later he was himself eventually to serve as a missionary. The first missionary appointed was John Sergeant who had studied in Edwards' home and at one time courted one of the Edwards girls! Edwards kept up contacts with the mission over the years, and in 1743 he was named as a recipient for funds Sergeant was collecting for a school he was planning for Indian children.

At least one of his church members, Job Strong, became a missionary to the Indians. After a period of 'orientation' with John Brainerd (the brother of David), he was sent back to Northampton for more theological study under Edwards. Similarly, Gideon Hawley, who went out from Stockbridge as an itinerant missionary when Edwards was there, was profoundly influenced by Edwards and often returned from his missionary journeys to confer with him. On one of his journeys he took the young Jonathan Edwards Junior with him with a view to his learning the Indian language and eventually becoming a missionary himself. Edwards was no theoretical supporter of missions; he was willing to commit his son to what was a dangerous experience in order to further the cause of missionary work (He himself was too unwell for such itinerant work and confessed himself too old to learn the Indian language)

Jonathan Edwards' involvement in the work of editing David Brainerd's diaries for publication is well known. It is an undisputed fact that (with the exception of the Apostle Paul!) David Brainerd's diaries have been the most influential missionary biography ever published. More men and women have volunteered for missionary work and more jaded and discouraged missionaries have persevered in their work as a result of reading the diaries than has happened with any other similar work. Edwards' interest in Brainerd's missionary activities began long before he edited the dead man's journal for publication. His first contact came in 1743, after Brainerd had been interviewed by Aaron Burr, Edwards' son-in-law, and two other of Edwards' friends for missionary work among the Indians. At that time he supported Brainerd's petition to the Yale authorities for the granting of his degree (Brainerd had been expelled from Yale for unwise remarks about the spiritual state of one of the tutors!), and he continued his interest in succeeding years. In his letters to Scottish friends he told with joy of the spiritual awakening among the Indians through Brainerd's ministry and he also celebrated the fact with a special thanksgiving service in his congregation.

When Brainerd on his deathbed asked Edwards to edit his diaries for publication, he felt it to be so important that he put aside the work he was doing on *The Freedom of the Will* (which in his view was also of vital significance in the eighteenth century New England church situation) to give himself to the task. In August 1748 he wrote to John Erskine in Scotland, 'I have for the present, been diverted from the design I hinted to you, of publishing something against some of the Arminian Tenets, by something else that Divine Providence unexpectedly laid in my way, and seemed to render unavoidable, viz. publishing Mr. Brainerd's Life.'

Edwards is not a passive editor who merely lets the words of Brainerd speak for themselves. Throughout the work he provides notes explaining personal details and giving reasons for various movements recorded, especially those which have to do with the Indian mission, disclosing something of the strategy and planning behind the work. In the 'Appendix Containing Some Reflections and Observations on the Preceding Memoirs of Mr Brainerd' he draws out lessons in Brainerd's life and experience. He obviously wants to use Brainerd's life as an object lesson in true spirituality as he (Edwards) has expounded it in various of his other writings. However, he also wants to use it to portray the sort of men who should be chosen as missionaries in the future, as well as giving guidance on the actual conduct of missionary work.

He says at one point, 'it may be of direction ... as to the proper qualifications of missionaries'. They should be, like Brainerd, those with a clear conversion experience, who evidence growth in holiness, and who are free from the excesses of 'enthusiasm'. Brainerd's whole-hearted commitment to the work is used as an example to 'us who are called to the work of ministry, and all that are candidates for that great work'; but, especially, 'his example of labouring, praying, denying himself ... may afford instruction to missionaries in particular.'

> He in his whole course acted as one who had indeed sold all for Christ and had entirely devoted himself to God, and made his glory his highest end, and was fully determined to spend his whole time and strength in his service.

> One practical point about which he

> would take occasion from the foregoing history to mention and propose to the consideration of such as have the care of providing and sending missionaries among savages; viz. whether it would not ordinarily be best to send two together?

He blames the fact of Brainerd's 'melancholy', which troubled him so often and so deeply, on the fact of his being alone under such difficult conditions, and quotes Brainerd's own words to him on the subject while he lay dying in the Northampton parsonage. Jonathan Edwards was obviously concerned for the spiritual and psychological well-being of those who were called as missionaries.

During the final months of Brainerd's life, which he spent in Edwards' home, much of Edwards' time was taken up with the preparation of another book for publication, the *Humble Attempt*. This work, as its full title suggests *(An Humble Attempt to Promote Explicit Agreement and Visible Union of God's People in Extraordinary Prayer, For the Revival of Religion and the Advancement of Christ's Kingdom on Earth, pursuant to Scripture-Promises and Prophecies concerning the Last Time)* is a call to Christians to join together in prayer for revival and the spread of the Gospel. It shows Edwards as a man of deep spiritual insight and trust in God, who believes that the work of missions is God's work and one of our main tasks is to pray.

The *Humble Attempt* also contains Jonathan Edwards' theological understanding of God's purposes for the future, and this, together with a series of sermons he preached over ten years earlier (and which were published after his death under the title *A History of the Work of Redemption*) and another work which was also published posthumously, show his grand vision of the purposes of God from eternity to eternity, in which missions have a key place.

'Man's chief end is to glorify God and to enjoy him forever.' So says the Westminster Shorter Catechism, which Jonathan Edwards had been taught as a child himself and which he valued highly throughout his life. '**God's** chief end is to glorify himself with a view to bringing man to enjoy him forever' may serve as a summary of Edwards' understanding of 'the End for which God created the World' (the title of the posthumous work referred to above which provides the background against which to understand his theology of mission). 'God glorifies Himself towards the creatures [in] two ways: 1. By appearing to them, being manifested to their understanding. 2. In communicating Himself to their hearts, and in their rejoicing, and delighting in, and enjoying, the manifestations which He makes of Himself.' So God is glorified when his rational creatures enjoy his love and respond to him in worship, love and obedience. And this is the chief end of God in creation. The great work of redemption which God planned before creation, and which he has been at work to accomplish since the Fall, culminating in the death of Christ, is concerned with the outworking of his purpose to glorify himself in this way. Through the centuries of God's dealings with Abraham and his descendants the majority of mankind were left in darkness and sin, but since the death and resurrection of the Saviour and the coming of the Holy Spirit at Pentecost, the work of redemption in its outworking embraces the world. And the greatest extension of the kingdom of Christ in the world is still in the future, according to Edwards.

Jonathan Edwards may be classed as post-millennial in his view of the future. In other words he believed in the conversion of the whole world, including the people of Israel, before the Second Coming of Christ. This view is strictly in the minority today, but we should not immediately reject Edwards' ideas as outdated and irrelevant. While we may not agree with his views (many Christians are not even aware of such views!), we can catch something of the excitement and God-centred optimism which Edwards has, and without necessarily accepting the post-millennial position outright we may have a similar confidence in the power of God and expect greater success in the preaching of the Gospel before the Return of Christ than we often do.

Writing in the first half of the eighteenth century, Edwards had very little Protestant missionary work to record. However, he had lived through two periods of general revival, one from 1734 to 1735 which affected at least thirty towns in the Connecticut River Valley and the second from 1740 to 1742 which had affected the whole of New England as well as the Middle Colonies. He knew of parallel revivals in Britain and Continental Europe and he became increasingly convinced that the next event in God's timetable was a further 'glorious work of God's Spirit by which Satan's kingdom is to be overthrown', and which would result in the revival of the spirit of true Christianity, the abolition of heresy, the overthrow of the Papacy and the power of Islam, the conversion of the Jews and the spread of the Gospel to the utmost parts of the world. All of this would happen, he believed, 'very swiftly, yet gradually'. Even if it began immediately, says Edwards, it would probably not be completed before the year 2000. Where it will begin, or whether it will begin in many places at the same time, is unknown, but the result will be that multitudes will turn from vice and wickedness and that 'vital religion' will revive. Conversions will take place on a scale hitherto unknown.

The Holy Spirit will equip men to be his instruments for carrying on this work, giving them knowledge and wisdom, and 'fervent zeal for the promoting of the Kingdom of Christ, and the salvation of souls, and propagating the gospel in the world'. Through the preaching of the gospel 'vast multitudes [shall be brought] savingly home to Christ'.

> That work of conversion shall go on in a wonderful manner, and spread more and more...The gospel shall be preached to every tongue, and kindred, and nation, and people...it will soon be gloriously successful to bring in multitudes from every nation.
>
> Some shall be converted, and be the means of the conversion of others.... And doubtless one nation shall be enlightened and converted after another, one false religion and false way of worship exploded after another.

It will not be without 'violent and mighty opposition', for:

> When the Spirit begins to be so gloriously poured forth, and the devil sees such multitudes flocking to Christ in one nation and another ... it will greatly alarm all hell.

All the forces of Antichrist, Mahometanism, and heathenism will be united, and oppose the spread of the gospel through persecution and other kinds of opposition, but this will be overcome 'by his word and Spirit'. Jewish unbelief will come to an end and Israel will accept Jesus as their Messiah, and the heathen nations will be 'wonderfully enlightened with the glorious gospel' as 'many shall go forth and carry the gospel unto them'. An extended citation is worthwhile at this point to show something of Edwards' vision for the conversion of the non-Christian world:

Then shall the many nations of Africa, the nations of Negroes, and other heathens who chiefly fill that quarter of the world, who now seem to be in a state but little above the beasts, and in many respects much below them, be enlightened with glorious light, and delivered from all their darkness, and shall become a civil, Christian, understanding, and holy people. Then shall the vast continent of America, which now in so great a part of it is covered with barbarous ignorance and cruelty, be everywhere covered with glorious gospel light and Christian love; and instead of worshipping the devil, as now they do, they shall serve God, and praises shall be sung everywhere to the Lord Jesus Christ, the blessed Saviour of the world. So may we expect it will be in that great and populous part of the world, the East Indies, which are now mostly inhabited by the worshippers of the devil; and so throughout that vast country Great Tartary: and then the kingdom of Christ will be established in those continents which have been more lately discovered towards the north and south poles, where now men differ very little from the wild beasts, excepting that they worship the devil, and beasts do not. The same will be the case with respect to those countries which have never yet been discovered.

There is no suggestion in Edwards' mind that the millennium itself would begin in his lifetime; indeed an amazing and unparalleled progress would be necessary, even if the work began immediately (he was writing in 1747), for it to be completed by the year 2000, as he goes on to explain:

Would it not be a great thing, to be accomplished in one half century, that religion, in the power and purity of it, should so prevail, as to gain the conquest over all those many things that stand in opposition to it among Protestants, and gain the upper hand through the Protestant world? And if in another [half century], it should go on so to prevail, as to get the victory over all the opposition and strength of the kingdom of Antichrist, so as to gain the ascendant in that which is now the popish world? And if in a third half century, it should prevail and subdue the greater part of the Mahometan world, and bring in the Jewish nation, in all their dispersions? And then in the next whole century, the whole heathen world should be enlightened and converted to the Christian faith, throughout all parts of Africa, Asia, America, Terra Australis, and be thoroughly settled in Christian faith and order, without any remainders of their old delusions and superstitions, and this attended with an utter extirpation of the remnant of the Church of Rome, and all the relics of Mahometanism, heresy, schism and enthusiasm, and a suppression of all remains of open vice and immorality, and every sort of visible enemy to true religion, through the whole earth, and bring to an end all the unhappy commotions, tumults, and calamities occasioned by such great changes, and all things so adjusted and settled through the world, that the world thenceforward should enjoy an holy rest or sabbatism.

At the same time, he certainly hoped that the Great Awakening would be the first of a series of revivals which would gradually spread worldwide and so at least begin the process. In February 1740 he wrote to George

Whitefield inviting him to visit Northampton as part of his tour of New England. His letter is full of hope that the current movement of the Spirit would, in fact, herald the hoped-for world-wide awakening. His words are exuberant as he encourages the young preacher:

> May you go on Rev. Sir! and may God be with you more and more abundantly, that the work of God may be carried on by a Blessing on your Labours still, with that Swift Progress that it has been hitherto, and rise to a greater height, and extend further and further, with an irresistable Power bearing down all opposition! and may the Gates of Hell never be able to prevail against you! *and may God send forth more Labourers into his Harvest of a Like Spirit, until the Kingdom of Satan shall shake, and his proud Empire fall throughout the Earth and the Kingdom of Christ, that glorious Kingdom of Light, holiness, Peace and Love, shall be established from one end of the Earth unto the other!* [emphasis added]

Writing in 1742 (in *Some Thoughts Concerning the present Revival of Religion in New England*), he expresses the same hope:

> 'Tis not unlikely that this work of God's Spirit that is so extraordinary and wonderful, is the dawning, or at least a prelude, of that glorious work of God, so often foretold in Scripture, which, in the progress and issue of it, shall renew the world of mankind.

Before we dismiss Edwards' speculations as discredited and disproved by the rampant evil we see all around us and by the size of the missionary task that still remains to be done, as well as by the millions who follow one of the great non-Christian religions of the world, or no religion at all, we need to remember certain facts about the world and the Church since Edwards' day. A succession of local revivals continued to break out in Britain, Europe and the United States even after the more widespread awakening ceased. These merged into what is generally known as the Second Great Awakening (in American usage) or the Second Evangelical Revival (in British usage), which lasted from 1792 till around 1840. This produced the beginnings of the modern Protestant missionary movement which grew and developed at an amazing rate throughout the nineteenth century (often referred to as 'the Great Century of Missions'). Further significant revivals occurred in mid-century (the so-called 'Prayer Revival' because of the prominence of prayer meetings led by lay people) as well as in the 1880s and most significantly in the first decade of the twentieth century. The years 1900-1910 saw the Welsh Revival and the birth of modern Pentecostalism. What is often not realized is that these were the most significant of multitudes of local and often regional revivals, not only in Britain, Europe and the United States, but worldwide in the scores or hundreds of places that the Church had been planted in the course of the previous century. Two World Wars and the Cold War that followed, together with various regional crises and world economic recession have captured the headlines, but the Church has known unprecedented growth and renewal, especially in the last forty years. Pentecostalism, charismatic renewal, evangelical growth and influence in the old Protestant Churches, dramatic changes in the Roman Catholic Church, these all bear witness to the power of the Spirit's work in the Church of Jesus Christ. Jonathan Edwards may himself not have been happy with every movement mentioned here but his hope of a succession of revivals and awakenings has been fulfilled in an amazing way.

In 1750 Jonathan Edwards was dismissed from his pastorate at Northampton where he had been for nearly twenty-five years. He spent the last seven years of his life as the pastor of a small white congregation on the frontier at Stockbridge and as a missionary to the Indians there. It has often been suggested that he accepted the post in order to get on with his writing and only paid scant attention to his missionary and pastoral responsibilities. This is completely untrue; he combined all three of these tasks and did not neglect any of them. He was particularly conscientious in his missionary task and preached, pastored, catechized and cared for the physical as well as the educational and spiritual needs of the Indians. He protected them from the greedy land-grabbing activities of the Whites, writing numerous letters to try and get these illegal activities stopped. He also developed plans for further evangelizing the Indian tribes more distant from Stockbridge, and he showed great courage when the settlement was threatened by war and attack.

It was with great reluctance that he accepted a call to become president of the New Jersey College (later Princeton) and he left Stockbridge in tears.

Lessons for today

His greatness was only partly recognized during his lifetime, but his influence in a multitude of ways continues up to the present. Through his writings on prayer and revival the Second Awakening began a generation after his death and in countless ways the Church of Christ has reason to thank God for the work of Jonathan Edwards. We, similarly, need to be faithful to the Lord in what he calls us to do and leave the results and our reputations in his hands.

5

COUNT ZINZENDORF
(1700 – 1760)

Engagement in Mission

Nikolaus Ludwig, Graf von Zinzendorf and Pottendorf, an eighteenth-century German nobleman – who was he and what has he to do with world missions? Far more than all the other Christian leaders we have mentioned thus far! They *wrote* about world mission but he engaged in it and, in fact, was the leader of a denomination which was one hundred per cent committed to world mission at a time when other Protestants were doing little or nothing about the world outside Europe. In fact, the pioneering attempts that we have been looking at so far, which produced no more than a trickle of cross-cultural missionaries, hardly prepare us for the veritable flood of missionary activity that we meet when we come to study the work of the *Moravian Church*. This group, formed in the 1720s from a number of refugees from religious persecution, who were given a plot of land on the estates of a young, recently married Pietist count in southeastern Saxony, seemed no different from many similar groups who were seeking religious freedom at a time of great population shifts in Central Europe following the Treaty of Westphalia in 1648.

However, within ten years of their arrival in 1722 they sent out their first missionaries to the West Indies; in 1733 two more went to Greenland to work among the Eskimos. By the turn of the century, hundreds had gone out, many of whom had died, others had returned for various reasons, and a total of 160 were still serving in places as far apart as India, South Africa, South America, North America and Labrador. Who were these people, what was their motivation, how did they work, what results did they achieve; what difference was there between them and other Protestant groups; what effect did they have on the much larger and widespread Protestant missionary movement which began sixty years later?

The nobleman who gave them shelter on his estate was Nikolaus Ludwig, Count and Lord of Zinzendorf and Pottendorf. The core of the refugees were the remnants of the *Unitas Fratrum* or Unity of Brethren, which had been formed in Bohemia in 1457 (sixty years before Luther nailed his ninety-five theses to the door of the church in Wittenberg), but who since 1620 had been hounded and persecuted by the Jesuits in the Habsburg Empire (See chapter 1). When, in 1727, the group had a renewing experience of the Holy Spirit (which was also happening in a number of other places in Central Europe at the time), the result was an explosion of spiritual life and activity which produced, among other things, the Moravian missionary movement.

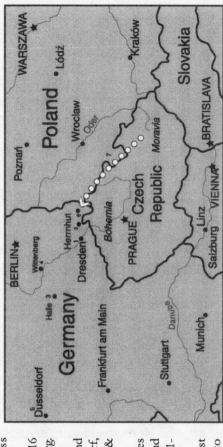

1. Zinzendorf born in Dresden. 1700

2. Early years in Gross Hennersdorf.1700-1710

3. Educated at Halle. 1710-1716

4. Studied law at Wittenberg. 1716-1719

5. Educational trip. 'The Grand Tour' including Dusseldorf, Holland, France & Switzerland.1719-1921

6. Returns to Saxony. Takes office in Dresden, mairries and settles in Berthesdorf. 1721-1722

7. Christian David leads first group of Moravians to Berthesdorf. 'Herrnhut' established

Count Zinzendorf

Zinzendorf was a complex character, who inspired extremes of both loyalty and opposition.

He was born in Dresden, Saxony, on 26 May 1700. His grandfather had been a Protestant refugee who had left Austria in 1661, so Zinzendorf had personal affinities with the refugees from Moravia and Bohemia whom he later sheltered. His father, who had become a privy councillor in Saxony, died in the year Nikolaus was born, and in 1703 his widowed mother joined her mother, Baroness Henrietta Catherine von Gersdorf at her estate of Grosshennersdorf near Zittau. When she remarried four years later, young Nikolaus was left in the care of his maternal grandmother and of his aunt Henrietta Sophie, who was fifteen years his senior. Baroness von Gersdorf was a champion of Pietism (the renewal movement in the Lutheran Church which began in the previous century), and, in fact, persuaded Philip Jakob Spener, founder of the movement, who was a frequent visitor to the castle, to be godfather to her young grandson. She and her brothers-in-law supported August Hermann Francke in the difficult days of his early work at Halle. She also had a number of Slav serfs on her estate, who were periodically joined by other refugees from Bohemia, so again, Zinzendorf had her example before him when in 1722 he extended hospitality to the remnants of the *Unity* from Moravia and Bohemia.

Nikolaus' spiritual growth, which began very early, was nourished by Halle Pietism, and, although his own time at Halle was not entirely happy, and, in spite of the fact that he diverged in a number of areas from the emphases of Pietism, the Pietistic influence remained a major one in his life and thinking. Letters from Ziegenbalg and Plütschau the Pietist missionaries in Tranquebar were read at Grosshennersdorf, where Zinzendorf grew up and he also had the opportunity to meet both Plütschau and Ziegenbalg during his time at Halle, when the missionaries were home on furlough.

The *collegia pietatis* [Note: The Latin phrase *ecclesiola in ecclesia* – a little church within a church – was also used by Pietists to describe their groups] or small groups of committed Christians, which, were an essential part of Spener's programme of reform, were the model for Zinzendorf's efforts, even while at Halle in his early teens, to gather groups of boys together for prayer and testimony. Before he left Halle at the age of sixteen, he gave Francke a list of seven such associations that he had formed. The groups met in students' rooms, and in other secluded places. One such group contained Zinzendorf and four friends, including Frederick von Watteville, whose friendship and practical associations were to continue in later years. Out of the groups emerged what eventually became known as 'The Order of the Grain of Mustard Seed'. This was a compact of like-minded friends, who agreed together to adopt certain Christian standards of conduct, to seek the welfare of others at all times, and (importantly for our purposes) to work for the conversion of the Jews and the heathen. It was Zinzendorf's 'obligation' as a 'knight' of the Order which caused him to give refuge to the Czech *Unity* when he was informed of their plight.

In 1723, together with von Watteville and two other friends who were Lutheran ministers, Zinzendorf entered into 'The Covenant of the Four Brethren'. This was basically a renewal of the Order of the Grain of Mustard Seed, but with more specific aims, namely, to establish centres of vital godliness along Pietist lines. They covenanted together to seek the power of the Holy Spirit for their own spiritual renewal and for an increasing acceptance of the rule of Christ throughout the land. They aimed to use personal correspondence, to enlist clergymen to promote spiritual awakening, to print and publish devotional literature, to work for the reform of pastoral methods and the inner life of the church, to support itinerant evangelists, and to found a Christian College with distinct educational methods. Dresden, Gorlitz and Berthelsdorf were to be the first centres for these activities. When the spiritual renewal of the old Unity took place in 1727, Zinzendorf hoped that they would be a *collegium pietatis*, an *ecclesiola in ecclesia* for the renewal of the Lutheran Church in Saxony and further afield. Messengers went from Herrnhut, either singly or in pairs, to establish centres of fellowship and renewal. In Zinzendorf's terminology, they were members of the *Diaspora* among the churches, laymen and laywomen acting as leaven to influence the wider church. Five years later, similar pairs of missionaries would begin to go out to the wider 'heathen world'.

The old Unity of Brethren

The ancient Unity of Brethren, from which the first refugees at Herrnhut came, traced its roots to the medieval protests of a number of preachers and writers, the most notable of whom was Jan Hus, the Bohemian reformer martyred in AD 1415. During the national revolution which followed Hus' death, a small group of earnest Christians, among whom was included the nephew of the reforming Archbishop of Prague, John Rokycana, consulted with a radically minded farmer from the south of Bohemia, Peter Chelcicky, and on his advice, formed themselves into a fellowship which, in 1457, became the Unity of Brethren.(See the extended note at the end of Chapter 1.) Under Brother Luke of Prague (1458-1528), who became a leading bishop in the Unity, and is often described as its 'second founder', contacts with Martin Luther developed, and, possibly as a result of these, the Brethren in their confessions laid great stress on the universal priesthood of all believers.

Following the Battle of the White Mountain in 1620, when the Czech Protestant armies suffered a crushing defeat at the hands of the Catholic forces, all the clergy of the Unity were forced to leave the Habsburg lands, going into exile in Poland and elsewhere. The believers who remained continued to practise their faith in spite of constant harrying by the Jesuits. For over a century, the 'Hidden Seed' or 'The Quiet Ones in the Land', as they were called, were forced to rely on their own spiritual resources without 'benefit of clergy'. We are told that as those who left Bohemia and Moravia crossed the mountains into Poland they sang

> Naught have we taken with us,
> All to destruction is hurled,
> We have only our Kralitz Bibles
> And our 'Labyrinth of the World'.

This is what those who remained also possessed: the excellent translation of the Bible into Czech with explanatory notes (although the smaller, portable editions did not have annotations), and Jan Amos Comenius' spiritual allegory, the *Labyrinth of the World* which, following its publication in 1623, became a devotional classic (See Chapter 1 and the note on Further Reading). These books, together with others which survived the determined 'search and destroy' tactics of the Jesuits for all books proscribed by the papal 'Index', nourished the faith of the 'Hidden Seed' in those long, dark years.

There were other elements of their heritage which may also have prepared them in unique ways to be the Protestant missionary 'trailblazers'. It is worth spending time on these because, although apparently remote in time from the renewal of the Unity in Herrnhut in the 1720s, they were of key significance in preparing the group for their task of being the Protestant 'trailblazers' in the matter of world mission. Just as the Reformers' basic universal ecclesiology provided the theological undergirding for the missionary understanding of Carey, so the emphases in the Czech Reformation and the subsequent development was a necessary foundation for the missionary thought and activity of the Moravians. In the view of the present writer, the contribution of the Brethren's background was as decisive as that of Zinzendorf. He retained far more of the Lutheran state Church concept in his thinking, even when it was modified by the Pietistic influence and this may have seriously inhibited the form of missionary activity he engaged in had it not been for the influences of the Czech Brethren. Their experience of being already uprooted from their home soil meant that they were ready to continue to move out as 'strangers and pilgrims'.

The beginnings of Herrnhut

In 1717 Christian David (1691-1751), a carpenter by trade, but a man with a varied career, and with considerable spiritual experience who had himself been influenced by the revivals in Silesia, began an itinerant preaching ministry in Moravia, visiting and encouraging the 'Hidden Seed'. An awakening occurred in 1720, around Litomysl and Litice in Bohemia, and also in Moravia, in the areas where the secret believers were particularly numerous. In both areas there was brutal repression, and persecution was particularly severe in Bohemia, where some of the Brethren were guilty of excesses. When Christian David met Zinzendorf, he told him of the plight of the believers in Moravia and Zinzendorf said to him, 'Let as many as will of your friends come hither. I will give them land to build on, and Christ will give them the rest.' Soon after, in 1722, the first ten refugees from Sehlen in Moravia arrived with Christian David, and settled on Zinzendorf's estate. They arrived while Zinzendorf was away, but they were given a plot of land and when the count returned he welcomed them. Over the next three years, the number from Moravia grew to ninety, and soon after, through the continued visits of David, a stream of refugees from Bohemia began to join them. A survey undertaken in 1756 found that nearly two thousand of Moravian or

Bohemian extraction had joined the Renewed Unity in the first thirty-four years.

Among the comparatively early arrivals at Herrnhut were five young men from Zauchental in Moravia, who, in 1724, stopped off at the new settlement in Saxony on their way to Leszno in Poland where there was a large settlement of Bohemian members of the Unity and where Comenius had lived for many years. Having experienced the power of the revival which had occurred a few years before, they were resolved to bring about the resuscitation of the Unity in Poland. However, they were so impressed with what was going on at Herrnhut that they stayed, and became leading figures in the life of the new group. They were all men of outstanding calibre, destined to have great influence in the Renewed Unity.

A decisive spiritual event took place on 13 August 1727, the day which the Moravian Church commonly reckons to be its 'birthday'. It was the 'day of the outpouring of the Holy Spirit upon the Congregation', 'its Pentecost', in the words of Zinzendorf. 'Then were we baptized by the Holy Spirit Himself to one love', according to August Gottlieb Spangenberg, Zinzendorf's successor; 'from that time on Herrnhut became a living Congregation of Christ', according to the testimony of David Nitschmann, another of the early leaders. Christian David wrote: 'It is truly a miracle of God that out of so many kinds and sects as Catholic, Lutheran, Reformed, Separatist, Gichtelian and the like, we could have been melted into one.' The experience of the Holy Spirit which occurred during a confirmation service for two girls from Herrnhut at the parish church at Berthelsdorf was similar in nature to a number of other revivals taking place in the surrounding area. However, the results were far more widespread and long lasting, as we shall see. It really marks the beginning of the worldwide outreach of the Moravian Church.[1]

The renewed community at Herrnhut soon became the sending centre of what became known as the *Diaspora*, the scattering of the witnesses of the renewal, messengers going out singly or in pairs to establish centres of fellowship and new life in Germany, Austria and beyond. These witnesses were laymen, and laywomen, whose qualifications were a living experience of 'heart religion', focused on 'the Lamb of God'. In the same year (1727), two of the Nitschmann brothers were sent by the community at Herrnhut to Copenhagen, to initiate enquiries concerning the group's possible participation in missionary work. Five years later, in 1732, the first two missionaries, both laymen, left for the island of St Thomas in the West Indies, to work among the slaves. The following year, the first Moravians set out for Greenland – the missionary movement had begun.

The organization of the group had begun well before the renewing experience of August 1727, made necessary by the increasing problems being experienced, both among the refugees and from outside. As many other religious refugees, not only from Moravia and Bohemia, but from other parts of Central Europe, joined the community, tensions and disagreements threatened to destroy the whole experiment. Criticisms from outside that Zinzendorf was harbouring a nest of heretics on his estate were exacerbated by the demands from Pastor Rothe of nearby Berthelsdorf that all the members of the community should accept the Augsburg Confession and become Lutherans. In 1726 an apocalyptic firebrand, by the name of Kruger, further disrupted the group. From that year Zinzendorf, as Squire of Berthelsdorf, devoted considerable time away from his state post in Dresden in trying to promote unity among the diverse groups on his estate. He gradually assumed a role of spiritual leadership in the new community, spending whole nights and days in conversation and counsel with them.

In February 1725, a distinctive feature based on the practice of the Unity of Brethren, from whom the groups from Moravia and Bohemia derived, had already begun to develop. According to Zinzendorf:

> Helpers were appointed from among the loyal souls of the Congregation, for exhortation, for observance of the work, for service and almsgiving, for visiting the sick, and particularly for the guidance of souls.

Frederick Von Watteville, a friend of the Count from Halle days, was appointed to watch over the souls of the men, and his young bride was appointed over the women. Mordelt, a tailor from Berthelsdorf, was made a 'teacher', and Gottfried Hahn, also a local man, was appointed an 'overseer'. Three of the original refugees from Moravia, George Jaeschke with Jacob Neisser and his wife Anna, were appointed 'exhorters'; Augustine Neisser became an 'almoner'; and Christian David, Anna-Lena, a girl cowherd, and Gottlob, a lame young man, were given the office of 'nurse' to comfort the sick.

In April 1727 Zinzendorf resigned his government position and moved from Dresden to Berthelsdorf, in order to heal the various discords which were in danger of splintering the whole group. He told the group that, whereas Rothe would remain in full charge at Berthelsdorf, he himself would be responsible for the settlement as the assistant pastor (unordained) and catechist. Many of the divisions were healed, but those members who had come from the ancient *Unitas* were unwilling to become Lutherans. A compromise was reached, whereby Herrnhut was constituted as a civic community, as well as a spiritual community, and was further recognized as an *ecclesiola in ecclesia* within the parish church at Berthelsdorf, with special recognition being granted to the apostolic discipline and fellowship of the ancient Unity.

On 12 May Zinzendorf presented the community with the 'Manorial Injunctions and Prohibitions' which were to regulate the life of Herrnhut as a civic community, and then 'The Brotherly Agreement of the Brethren from Bohemia and Moravia and Others, Binding Them to Walk According to the Apostolic Rule'. The whole group accepted this and it was felt that a significant step forward had been taken. Twelve elders were elected to watch over the faithful observance of the forty-two statutes of the 'Brotherly Agreement'. Men of high rank and learning were excluded from the office, so that it might be filled by persons of the common class in whom all could have confidence. Among those chosen were a joiner, a weaver, a carpenter and a cobbler. The Count was chosen as Warden, and Frederick Von Watteville as his assistant: together with the elders, they watched over every detail of the temporal and spiritual life of the Settlement. Ministry was exercised by all who had the necessary gifts.

On 19 July and the following week, the 'Bands' came into existence. Without these, according to Zinzendorf, 'the Brethren's Church would never have become what it was'. A Band consisted of up to eight persons of some spiritual affinity who met together regularly to talk about their spiritual state and to encourage and pray for one another. The whole community was organized in this way, and one person appointed at the head of each group. There was a certain amount of rotation in the composition of the groups, so that gradually each person became acquainted with everyone else in the community. Eventually, ninety such groups were meeting twice a week for prayer and fellowship.

Zinzendorf's work as the unordained catechist grew, as he visited, encouraged, taught, and prayed with members of the community, either singly, in families, or in groups. Various groups, both large and small, met together frequently for special prayer, often involving night-long vigils. Zinzendorf was away for about two weeks, during which time he discovered in the Zittau Library a copy of the *Ratio Disciplinae* of Comenius. He found, to his delight, that the 'Statutes' which he had drawn up bore a strong resemblance to the ancient Discipline. When he returned to Herrnhut, he shared his findings with the Brethren, and all felt that this was divine confirmation of the rightness of what they were doing. The spiritual experience of August 13, which soon followed, was the climax of the months and years of struggle that had gone before.

Two weeks later, twenty-four brethren and twenty-four sisters covenanted together to spend one hour each, day and night, in prayer for the divine blessing on the Congregation and its witness. Thus began, on lay initiative, as was the case with virtually everything in the beginnings of the Moravian Church, the 'Hourly Intercession', which spread as the Moravian witness spread, and which continued for over a hundred years.

In 1728 the 'Choir' system began, partly through the suggestion of Zinzendorf, the *Vorsteher*, or *Ordinarius*, as he was known, and partly through the initiative of the members of the Community themselves.[2] The Congregation was divided into ten 'Choirs' or groups, according to sex, age, and marital status. There was an Elder or Labourer over each Choir, an Eldress in the case of the single Sisters. The single Brethren moved into their own Choir House in 1728, with Martin Linner, a baker, as their Elder. In 1730 the single Sisters occupied their Choir House for the first time, with the fifteen-year-old Anna Nitschmann as their Eldress.[3] (In 1756 Zinzendorf's first wife died and a year later he married Anna Nitschmann.) The Labourer of each Choir reported to Zinzendorf and the Elders of the whole community each week on the spiritual state of the members of his or her Choir. The children in their Choirs and schools and orphanages were the responsibility of the whole community, and their parents, far away on the mission field, knew that their children were being lovingly cared for. Indeed, the whole community was like an army in training[4], prepared and ready to serve the Lamb whenever a call came, and ready to replace any missionary who died, or for any reason returned home.

In the words of the great missions historian, Kenneth Scott Latourette:

> Here was a new phenomenon in the expansion of Christianity, an entire community, of families as well as of the unmarried, devoted to the propagation of the faith. In its singleness of aim it resembled some of the monastic orders of earlier centuries, but these were made up of celibates. Here was a fellowship of Christians, of laity and clergy, of men and women, marrying and rearing families, with much of the quietism of the monastery and of Pietism but with the spread of the Christian message as a major objective, not of a minority of the membership, but of the group as a whole.

Moravian distinctives, positive and negative

Before describing in more detail the missionary activity of the Church as it developed from 1732 onwards, it may be useful to bring together a number of the key emphases which characterized the Moravians. The beginnings of some of these have already been described, but they are worth underlining. The first of these is a strong Christo-centrism, focused particularly on the sufferings of Christ on the cross. Their **devotion to the Lamb of God** was seen in a number of ways. The seal of the Polish branch of the ancient *Unitas Fratrum* which was used on the certificate when Zinzendorf was consecrated as a Moravian bishop by Bishop Daniel Ernst Jablonski in 1737, inscribed with

112

a Lamb carrying a flag with the motto *'Vicit Agnus Noster, Eum Sequamur'* ('Our Lamb has conquered. Let us follow Him'), was taken over by the Renewed Moravian Church and made its own. It expressed concisely the focus of living and preaching of the community, both in its strengths and weaknesses. Derived as it was from Pietism, it was developed in Moravian thought and devotion in a thoroughly distinctive way. The 'blood and wounds' theology dominated, often in an unhealthy way, particularly in what is known as 'the Sifting Period' from around 1743 to 1750, when the worst excesses of bad taste in the language of devotion are seen. However, at its best, it is a thoroughly biblical emphasis, and it provided much of the motivation for sacrificial and often heroic missionary service of the early Moravians. The adoration and proclamation of the slaughtered Lamb was the centre and secret of Moravianism. Among the many hymns Zinzendorf wrote on the subject of Christ's sufferings, 'Jesus, Thy blood and righteousness', which is free from unscriptural excesses, can serve as a summary of his emphasis.

In their preaching also, they concentrated on the Cross, and found this so remarkably successful that they again made it a Moravian distinctive. The Moravian missionaries in Greenland were those who found it most strikingly effective, as the following account makes clear:

> As John Beck sat in his tent translating the Gospels into the native tongue, a group of Eskimos gathered round him. They asked him about his work, and he began, as he had often tried before, to open up the questions of dogmatic theology with them. But they

turned away. And then in an inspired moment, John Beck slowly read the verses he had just translated from St Matthew's account of the Agony in Gethsemane. 'And He took with him Peter and the two sons of Zebedee, and began to be sorrowful and very heavy. And He fell on His face and prayed, saying, "Father, if it be possible, let this cup pass from Me"'. Where argument had failed, the story of the Suffering Saviour prevailed – a lesson the Moravian missionaries never forgot. A young Eskimo, named Kayarnak, demanded with eager amazement: 'What is that? Tell me that again; for I too would be saved.' All that night the passion of the Lamb was told.

The result was a spiritual breakthrough and the first Eskimo converts, Kayarnak and his family.

Another distinctive feature of the Moravians was their **dependence on prayer.** We have already mentioned the twenty-four hour prayer watch which began in 1727 and continued for over a hundred years, together with the frequent prayer meetings of the bands and choirs. When the missionary work of the community began in earnest, it became the practice once a month to spend a whole day in reading the letters which arrived from missionaries in different parts of the world and in interceding for the work. At such times, when news of the death of any of the overseas workers was announced, or when the need for more workers became obvious, there was never any shortage in further volunteers. A further regular prayer day was the Jewish Day of Atonement, when, again, the whole day was spent in collective prayer for the conversion of the Jews.

The **tight discipline** of the community through the bands, choirs and the various offices of leadership, which was necessary for the community to function in the way it did, required a commitment from every member and a willingness for the interests of the group to take precedence over that of the individual member and his or her family. Zinzendorf was the frequent, although not the exclusive, channel through whom Christ was believed to show His will. The casting of lots was also used to receive guidance. When a member was about to make any major decision affecting their life, they were required to submit it to the decision of the community. This applied to such matters as taking a long journey! There is some evidence that in the American colonies, there were a number of members who rebelled against the strict discipline and control, particularly in the time of what was known as 'the General Economy'. However, it seems that in general, certainly in the early days, members were happy to be under such community guidance.

The positive aspect of the close-knit nature of the Moravian community was the experience of **fellowship**. The bands and the choirs with their regular patterns of prayer, worship and sharing, together with the fact that Herrnhut, and other Moravian groups modelled on it, were self-sufficient industrial and craft communities, all made for the strengthening of Christian love. As we have seen, the same features could also produce an esoteric and eccentric kind of behaviour, but even when this happened, any opposition which came from outside would serve to further strengthen the ties within the community. It has been said that the Moravians virtually made Fellowship a third Sacrament of the Church. A Moravian author comments: 'There is truth in this remark – for the Moravian, fellowship is a signal means of grace, as necessary as any Sacrament, and the practical cultivation of fellowship is an outward and visible act accompanied by an inner spiritual meaning.'

Every choir, which was ten in number, had its own Choir House where the members lived, worshipped and plied their trades. Each choir established its own 'Economy' or 'Diacony', an organization embracing trades, crafts, farming and joint housekeeping. Some prospered more than others, and some trading companies which grew out of the early Moravian activities still exist today. The whole enterprise was intended to support the spiritual work of the community, especially its missionary work. Wherever the Moravian missionaries went, they engaged in such activities, and while they did not always succeed in being completely self-supporting, they shouldered a considerable amount of the financial burden themselves.

Such communitarian Christian communities are not unique in Christian history, either before the establishment of the Moravians, or since, but they certainly were, and possibly still are, unique in being a Christian community where **the whole local church**, not just a keen minority, was devoted to a mission of renewal and unity to **the whole Christian Church**, and a mission of evangelism to **the whole world**.

The mission to the world was more successful than that to the whole Church. In Europe and America they were often opposed by the other denominations, especially the Lutheran Church, again, both in Europe and America. Zinzendorf often said that he did not want to form a new denomination, but merely be a leaven for renewal among the already existing Churches. He used the 'Diaspora' concept to describe the influence of the Moravians among the denominations, but also spoke of them as one 'Tropus' (from the Greek *tropos peideias* method of training) among the many Tropoi, with its own particular jewel of truth and insight into the riches of Christ. It may have been the ambiguous way in which Zinzendorf spoke of the Moravian relationship with the other Churches, or it may have been the sometimes eccentric behaviour of himself or his followers, at times it seems to have been the less-than-honest way Zinzendorf appeared to conduct his affairs, but the result often was opposition from other Christian leaders. He fell out with Gotthilf August Franke, the son of August Hermann Francke who took over the leadership at Halle. Johann Albrecht Bengel, the Pietist Biblical scholar at Württenberg, crossed swords with him. The Orthodox Lutherans and the Pietists opposed him, and more than once he was exiled from Saxony and other parts of the German Federation. John Wesley and George Whitefield, after initially friendly contacts, turned against the Moravians. (Wesley's experience of conversion/assurance came through Moravians, and he visited Herrnhut and other Moravian settlements in Germany soon after). Philip Doddridge, the peace-loving Independent minister, who had good fellowship with Zinzendorf for a time, later felt that there were aspects of Moravian belief and practice that he was unhappy with (especially when Moravians disrupted his own church fellowship!). Gilbert Tennent and the Presbyterians of the Middle Colonies opposed them (and seemed to have passed on their negative views to Jonathan Edwards, David Brainerd and other New England leaders). Henry Muilenberg, the Pietist Lutheran who was sent to America to organize the Lutheran Church there had a confrontation with Zinzendorf which marked the end of the count's attempts to unite all the German-speaking Christians in the American colonies under his banner. The 'apostle of unity' was singularly unsuccessful in this part of his mission!

However, in the pioneer trailblazing work of world mission, the Moravians were 'successful'. They established missions in many countries in an incredibly short time, and they provided a stimulus to many others, including most notably William Carey, to engage in similar work. To this work we now turn.

Moravian Missionary Work
In September 1727, a month after the powerful renewing experience of the Holy Spirit on the community, two of the Nitschmann brothers were dispatched to Copenhagen to enquire about the possibility of overseas missionary work, following the example of the Pietist mission in Tranquebar which had been sponsored by the Danish king. They were received by members of the Danish court and royal family, and returned with an account of the work which Hans Egede, another Pietist missionary, was doing in Greenland. On 10 February 1728, at the very first of the monthly congregational 'Prayer Days', the community determined to prepare itself for the task

of worldwide mission, and Zinzendorf presented a plan for evangelism in the West Indies, Greenland, Turkey and Lapland. The next day, twenty-six of the single men, under the leadership of Leonard Dober, made a covenant together to pray for the world mission of the Church and to go out immediately on receiving a clear call. Zinzendorf began to conduct classes for them in geography, writing, medicine and theology in preparation for the time when they would go. As we have seen already, Zinzendorf's theology was Christ-centred and Cross-centred. He also strongly emphasized justification by faith. In John Wesley's view, he did this to the neglect of the need for sanctification and good works. The count was very suspicious of the academic theology of Orthodox Lutheranism. He wrote: 'We believe that the whole theology needed to enable us to stand before the holy angels without shame can be written in big characters on an octavo sheet. Anyone who neglects this basic theology fails to experience salvation.'

In April 1731, Zinzendorf, accompanied by three Moravians, visited Copenhagen to attend the coronation of King Christian VI. While there, he heard that the government had recalled the soldiers and artisans who had been in Greenland with Hans Egede, and that the mission there was in imminent danger of collapse. He also met a Black slave from the Danish West Indies who told him of the dire conditions of slaves on the plantations there. When he returned to Herrnhut in July and told of his meeting, two of the brethren, Leonard Dober and Tobias Leupold, felt God's call to go to the West Indies, even if it meant becoming slaves themselves. Two others then voiced their willingness to go to Greenland. In both cases, Zinzendorf felt it wise to wait in order to test their call (at times he showed a wisdom in others' apparent leading which he failed to show in his own!), and the first two Moravian missionaries left on foot for Copenhagen on 21 August 1732 and sailed for the island of St Thomas on 8 October, arriving on 13 December. Dober was one and the other was not Leupold but David Nitschmann, who went out for a short time only in order to report back to Herrnhut on the need for more workers. Leupold and seventeen others arrived in June 1734, at which time Dober returned to take up the office of chief elder and taking with him the solitary convert from his first lonely eighteen months' work.

Some of the new group continued Dober's work on St Thomas, but others moved on to St Croix where the Danish authorities were planning to send slave labour. However, eight of the eighteen died of yellow fever before they could move on to St Croix, Tobias Leupold among them. In February a further eleven volunteers set out from Herrnhut, four of whom died in the next two months. During 1735 and 1736, most of the survivors returned to Herrnhut, all of them in very poor physical shape – and three of them were shipwrecked *en route*! However, in 1736 the spiritual harvest began to appear as hundreds of Dober's catechumens responded to the preaching of Friedrich Martin, who had arrived in March.

When Zinzendorf arrived for a visit in January 1739, he did not know of the blessings being experienced, nor of the problems that had overtaken Martin and his colleagues, who at that time were nearly starving to death in prison. As his boat entered the harbour, he said to Georg Weber, one of the early refugees from Moravia who had settled in Herrnhut, 'Suppose the brethren are no longer here; what shall we do?' Weber replied: 'In that case, we are here.' Zinzendorf's response was, '*Gens aeterna, diese Mähren!*' ('An indestructible race, these Moravians!') Zinzendorf secured the release of Martin and his companion, and spent time with the eight hundred Blacks who were regularly attending the worship services. He commented: 'St Thomas is a greater wonder than Herrnhut!' The work on St Croix continued to claim lives including, eventually, that of Friedrich Martin himself. He died of dysentery on a visit there in 1750. During his ministry of fourteen years he had preached 'the Lamb' to thousands and left behind a church of 425 among the slaves.

The first Moravian missionaries went to Greenland in 1733, including Christian David, although he soon fell out doctrinally with Egede! He returned to Herrnhut in 1735. Missions to Surinam, the Lapps of Sweden and the North American Indians all followed in 1735; the next year missionaries were sent to South Africa to work among the Hottentots and to the Gold Coast. In 1737 missionaries tried to reach the heathen tribes on the Arctic coast of Russia but were arrested as Swedish spies, imprisoned in St Petersburg and eventually released. In 1738 work was begun among the Blacks of North America and in 1740 the first Moravian missionaries arrived in Algeria and Ceylon. By that date, sixty-eight missionaries had been sent out from a community of no more than six hundred. The

'Dedication' in the Moravian *Text Book* for 1739 makes interesting reading:

> The Good Word of the Lord from all Prophets for His Congregation and Servants at Herrnhut, Herrnhag, Herrendyk, Pilgerruh, Ebersdorf, Jena, Amsterdam, Rotterdam, London, Oxford, Berlin [these were places where there were Moravian settlements or societies, and would count as *Diaspora* societies seeking to renew the Churches of Christendom], Greenland, St Croix, St Thomas, St Jan, Berbice, Palestine, Surinam, Savannah in Georgia, among the Negroes in Carolina, among the savages in Irene, in Pennsylvania, among the Hottentots, in Guinea, in Litvonia, and Esthonia, Lithuania, Russia, along the White Sea, Lapland, in Norway, in Switzerland, in Prison, on the journey to Ceylon, Ethiopia, Persia, on Visitation to the Messengers among the Heathen, and otherwise on Land and Sea.

By 1760, the year of Zinzendorf's death, a total of 226 had been sent out; of these a number had died, others had returned to Herrnhut (usually on orders from Zinzendorf or the elders). A total of twenty-eight countries had been entered in as many years. Sixty-six missionaries (forty-nine men and seventeen women) remained in thirteen stations. Worldwide around three thousand had been baptized; a total of 6,125 were under the care of the missionaries. In the West Indies the work had continued to grow after the death of Friedrich Martin; some 1,600 had been baptized, with around 3,600 under the care of the missionaries.

Missionary motivation, theology and strategy

Over the years, Zinzendorf produced at least fourteen pamphlets of 'Instructions' on mission affairs, including *A Letter to a Missionary of the English Society* (1732) written to an anonymous member of the Society for the Propagation of the Gospel; a specific set of *Instructions for the Georgia Colony* (1734); *Instructions for Missionaries to the East* (1736); a general set of *Instructions for all Missionaries to the Heathen* (1738), *The Right Way to Convert the Heathen* (1740); an outline *Plan for a Catechism for the Conversion of the Heathen (1744);* a sermon preached before a synod of the Moravian Church in Holland on *The Foundation of Our Mission to the Heathen* (1746), and *Homily for all Missionaries to Tranquebar* (1759). None of these is very extensive, because, as we have seen, the Count had a suspicion and dislike of intricate systems of academic theology, believing, rather, in 'radical simplicity in the Spirit'. However, it is possible from these, and from his *Nine Public Lectures* ... to construct the main lines of his theology of mission, its strategy and the motivation for mission it contains.

The primary motivation for mission for Zinzendorf and the Moravians was the love of God revealed in the Incarnation and supremely in the death of Jesus Christ, the Lamb of God. R. Pierce Beaver in a survey article on missionary motives comments:

> The primary motive of Moravian missions was the love of God in Christ, more than the glory of God. The glad celebration of the love of God and his gift of redemption in Christ called for the simple preaching everywhere of this story of salvation.

Compassion for the neglected, the despized, and the oppressed filled Moravian hearts, but did not generate the mission impulse. The salvation of perishing souls also was not a motive of any power with them.

The kingdom of God is also a factor in missionary motivation. According to Zinzendorf, the kingdom of God was the:

permanent action of God by means of angels and chosen people to universalize salvation, to facilitate the present order of salvation, to prepare for the third coming of the Saviour [presumably the 'second coming' was the coming of Christ the Bridegroom into the hearts of those who love him – a great emphasis of the count], to make people long for Him and to bring their hearts into an attitude pleasing to Him.

The command of Christ provides further motivation, although this was probably not as primary as the love of God. In *The Foundation of Our Mission to the Heathen* Zinzendorf quotes and paraphrases Christ's words:

Preach the gospel to all creatures, all nations ... no nation excepted, no people has preference here, no place in which they were born, not their language nor sex.

This was Christ's command which cannot be frozen into a particular period of history. It was 'the Saviour's own teaching method', to be remembered and followed.

The Church continually participates in this command throughout its history. Similarly, in the same year, when preaching in London on 'The Proper Purpose of the Preaching of the Gospel' he said:

> ... He wants to be looked at and to manifest Himself as the Saviour of all men. 'Go into all the world and preach the gospel to the whole creation' (Mark 16:15); whoever will now believe you, whoever will hold to me, whomever I will please, whoever will come to love me, he shall be saved; he shall be delivered from this present evil world and from the wrath to come and shall enter my rest. This then is the ground and purpose of the preaching of the Gospel plain and clear.

The missionary is to go into the world to find those in whom the Holy Spirit, Who is the great missionary, is already working. These 'Candace souls' or 'Cornelius souls' will listen to the word about the crucified Christ and will come to Him when He is 'lifted up'. In fact, according to Zinzendorf, the Spirit also works in many who do not hear the gospel preached outwardly, and draws them to Christ. For this he refers to Galatians 1:15-16, John 3:7-8, Luke 1:43 ff. These whom the Spirit brings to Christ, with or without the external preaching, are 'the first fruits', 'the bundles of the living', a 'lodge in the vineyard', or 'a holy beginning', terms taken from Scripture, e.g. Revelation 14:4; 1 Samuel 25:29.

In his letter of 1732 to an SPG missionary, he says that one should plan 'to work directly on no heathen in whom one does not find a happy disposition to a righteous nature because it is just they, e.g. Cornelius, the Ethiopian eunuch etc., to whom Christ sent his messengers', and in his *Instructions for Missionaries to the East* (1736) he says, 'Do not begin with public preaching but with a conversation with individual souls who deserve it, who indicate the Saviour to you, and you will perceive it. If it is desired of you, then also witness to each man the gospel publicly.' In his *Instructions to All Missionaries to the Heathen* (1738) he makes the same point: 'To our first missionaries to [St] Thomas, we gave the following instructions to take along: there to bring a soul to the Saviour and what else in addition the Saviour would want to give.' Those who requested baptism should be baptized if they believed in the Name of the Father, Son and Holy Spirit, and if they accepted a handful of basic elements of faith: firstly, 'a simple grasp of God become man through a miracle', including an outline of Jesus' earthly life and a knowledge that He became 'a sacrifice for the sins of the whole world with His own blood and death according to his accepted humanity', and that after His death 'he revived himself and has again ascended into heaven to feed his souls as a shepherd and feeds them and supports them daily through his spirit which we all feel, so that one can converse with him as with a friend'. Secondly, there was the need for a recognition of the difference between good and evil, of the fact that Satan and evil spirits control 'all those who do not know Jesus', and of the existence also of good spirits whom we cannot see; that we too are spirits clothed in flesh but after death our spirit will continue. There is also the need to understand the basic significance of baptism, 'a grasp that baptism aligns one with the blood of Christ, washes clean by God's order the nature of man of all sin, as a newly born child'. Finally, 'these concepts must abide with the baptized in a moved, bowed and sincere heart. The secrets of Holy Communion and all the other secrets remain unspoken to them until they, as our people, grow to understanding.'

In common with many Pietists, Zinzendorf did not expect large-scale conversions of the Gentiles until Israel turned to Christ; 'Large, national ... conversions to the slaughtered Lamb will be possible only when the devil will not be allowed to mislead the heathen any more.' Until that time, it is best to follow 'the timely method of the Saviour'. (In 1748 Moravian missionaries were sent to Amsterdam to work among the Jews there.) However, Zinzendorf and the Moravian missionaries were pleasantly surprised when, in many places, more than the ones and twos came to Christ, and the idea of the 'first fruits' was eventually abandoned. Among Zinzendorf's last words, he said, 'I only asked for first fruits among the heathen, and thousands have been granted to me.'

After Zinzendorf's death, a number of changes were made, especially in strategy. As the Moravians became increasingly a denomination, traditional patterns of growth and organization became standard among the missions. A contemporary Moravian, David Schattschneider also notes that Spangenberg, who succeeded Zinzendorf as acknowledged leader of the denomination, succeeded in making the doctrinal emphases less eccentric and distinctive, but probably at the cost of what he (Schattschneider) calls 'the demotion of the Spirit'. It is also a sad fact that Herrnhut exercised an over-heavy control of the overseas missions. In the case of the Moravian Church in the newly independent United States after independence from Britain was achieved, such control had a stifling effect on the work.

In spite of the mistakes, aberrations and excesses, however, the eighteenth century Moravian missionary effort was a notable chapter in the growth of Protestant missionary work and a stimulus to many others to take up such work for themselves.

Lessons for today

Zinzendorf and the Moravians were, as we have seen, a unique phenomenon in the history of Protestant missionary activity. However, they show many characteristics which reappear in Christian churches and para-church groups today. A group or organization which comes into existence from the vision or drive of a strong, gifted individual runs a strong risk of being controlled by that individual and following them in their failures and mistakes as well as in their God-given vision. The Moravians might have avoided some of the mistakes they made if someone had stood up to Zinzendorf more than they did. The same is true today. The example of the Moravians also shows that an individual or group whom God chooses to use may be far from perfect and in some respects rather eccentric! Those who seek to follow them in their good points should beware of imitating them in the excesses! Nevertheless, a church with no 'passengers', where every member is motivated and mobilized, can still do great things for God.

Notes:

[1.] See W.. R. Ward, *The Protestant evangelical awakening* Cambridge 1992 chapter 2

[2.] With many of the innovations of the early life of the Community, it is difficult to ascertain where the original initiative came from, whether from Zinzendorf and some of the other leaders, or from a larger number of the members of the Community. Whichever it was, there was a remarkable unanimity in the way the various ideas were accepted and implemented, which argues for the initiator(s) being very closely in touch with the feelings of the group as a whole. Furthermore, whether the suggestions came from the leader(s) or more spontaneously from the larger group, it was still a case of 'lay' initiative, as the whole group was composed of laymen and laywomen at the first.

[3.] At the same time, she was elected chief eldress of Herrnhut itself, and, later, of the Unity as a whole. She laid down her office temporarily in 1740, when she left for America, but resumed it later and continued in her position until her death.

[4] Much of the terminology used to describe the various functions and activities of individual offices within the community, as well as of the whole group was military in flavour.

CONCLUSION

Jonathan Edwards died in 1758 and Zinzendorf followed him two years later. As we have said, it was not for another thirty years or more, in 1792, that Protestants really began to get their act together and involve themselves in foreign missions. In that year William Carey published his little work *Enquiry into the Use of Means for the Conversion of the Heathen*, and the Baptist Missionary Society was formed, Carey himself going to India the next year as their first missionary.

Carey was influenced in different ways by all of the men we have been studying so far. He was extremely impressed by the missionary work of the Moravians, of whom Comenius was a forerunner and Zinzendorf a leader; Cotton Mather in his *Magnalia Christi Americana* provided the classical biography of John Eliot, the Puritan 'apostle to the [North American] Indians' which challenged Carey; Richard Baxter stimulated missionary interest in seventeenth-century England and influenced Philip Doddridge of Northampton where Carey and his friends were active. Most notably, Carey was deeply influenced by the writings of Jonathan Edwards, as were all his fellow-Baptists who shared his vision for missions. Edwards' *Freedom of the Will* helped Andrew Fuller, Carey and others to break free from the stifling Hyper-Calvinism which gripped most Baptists and other Nonconformists of the time; his sermons on *Justification by Faith* expounded this central truth with clarity over against Hyper-Calvinist ideas of 'eternal justification'; his *Religious Affections* and his other Revival writings showed the need for a personal experience of the New Birth and a warm-hearted relationship with the living Christ by the power of the Holy Spirit; his edition of *The Diary of David Brainerd* gave a stirring account of the missionary labour and personal sacrifice of the young missionary to the North American Indians which challenged Carey, and many like him, to go and to keep going in the face of the most extreme discouragements; his *History of the Work of Redemption* gave a post-millennial vision of the triumph of the Gospel over all unbelief through a succession of revivals and missionary activity; his *Humble Attempt to promote Explicit Agreement and Visible Union of God's People in Extraordinary Prayer for the Revival of Religion and the Advancement of Christ's Kingdom on Earth, pursuant to Scripture-Promises and Prophecies concerning the Last Time* reiterated this hope and connected it to the need for regular prayer on the part of Christians for this to happen. The story of how this last-named book of Edwards was the key factor in the beginning of the Protestant missionary movement has often been told, but bears repeating. The following pages are adapted from *Evangel EMA Occasional Paper No 3* Spring 1999. (See note on Further Reading):

In 1784 the Rev. John Erskine, a prominent Church of Scotland Evangelical who had been one of Edwards' Scottish correspondents, sent a copy of the *Humble Attempt* to the Northampton Baptist John Ryland Jr. In this work, Edwards had tried to encourage support for a proposal for a 'prayer concert' initiated by a group of Scottish Evangelical ministers by setting it into a biblical and eschatological framework using Zechariah 8:20-22. The *Humble Attempt* took the ideas of *The History of Redemption* one stage further and strongly suggested that persistent, united prayer is a major means which God has given to his people to prepare the way for Revival and the spread of the Gospel worldwide. The subsequent course of events show how this vision increasingly caught on among Evangelicals and resulted in the modern missionary movement.

When John Ryland Jr read the book that Erskine had sent him, he immediately passed it on to John Sutcliff in Olney, and then to Andrew Fuller in Kettering. Within a few days of reading it they, together with a few other colleagues, agreed to meet on the second Tuesday in every month 'to seek the revival of true religion, and the extension of Christ's kingdom in the world'. At the annual meeting of the Northamptonshire Association in Nottingham (the Northamptonshire Association included a number of churches in neighbouring counties), Andrew Fuller in his sermon called for his hearers to engage in 'earnest and united prayer for an outpouring of God's Spirit upon our ministers and churches, and not only upon our own connexion and denomination, but upon "all that in every place call upon the name of Jesus Christ our Lord, both theirs and ours"'. Sutcliff immediately followed this up by proposing to the association that there should be corporate prayer for one hour on the first Monday of each month 'to wrestle with God for the effusion of his Holy Spirit'. The delegates of the sixteen churches present agreed with enthusiasm and the Prayer Call was issued in June 1784. On 29 June

Sutcliff's church in Olney agreed to adopt the idea and the next month Andrew Fuller read a part of Edwards' *Humble Attempt* to his congregation to encourage them to do the same, which they did.

The following year, at its annual meeting, the churches of the Northamptonshire Association reaffirmed their commitment to the monthly prayer meetings, and in 1786 Sutcliff gave a progress report and further encouragement to continue. In the same year, the Midland Baptist Association made a similar commitment. By 1789 the number of prayer meetings had further increased and Sutcliff decided to republish Edwards' book to encourage even more. In his preface to the new edition he says, 'Many other churches, particularly in Yorkshire, have adopted, and now follow, the above practice', i.e. of 'a meeting of prayer for the general revival and spread of religion' on 'the first Monday of every calendar month'. He goes on, 'We have the pleasure also to find that several *Paedobaptist* churches statedly meet on those evenings for the same purpose.'

The practice soon spread to other countries. In 1787 in the United States, 'an Association of ministers' published their proposals for a Concert of Prayer. In 1792 Baptists in Boston adopted it, having been informed of what was happening in England, and in 1794 the veteran Baptist leader Isaac Backus and his friends began efforts to enlist support from all the major American denominations for the monthly concert of prayer. In 1798 the New York Missionary Society, a group comprising Baptists, Presbyterians and other Reformed Christians, summoned its members and friends on 'the second Wednesday evening of every month, beginning at candlelight' to united prayer to:

> 'the God of grace, that he would be pleased to pour his spirit on his Church, and send his gospel to all nations; and that he would succeed the endeavours of this Society, and all Societies instituted on the same principles, and for the same ends' (*New York Missionary Magazine* [1800], cited in R.P. Beaver 'The Concert of Prayer for Missions' in *Ecumenical Review* X [1957- 8] p. 427.)

In the same year in New England there were published:

> Circular letters, containing an invitation to every Christian denomination in the United States, to unite in their endeavors to carry into execution the 'Humble Attempt' of President Edwards, to promote explicit agreement...

In Britain in 1795, the directors of the newly formed London Missionary Society, formed by Evangelical Anglicans and Congregationalists, recommended that the prayer meeting on the first Monday of each month should be made a missionary prayer meeting. The idea met with immediate success, and prayer meetings in London began to proliferate. The practice then spread to 'all the principal cities and towns of the Kingdom', as well as to 'Holland, Switzerland, Germany, America, India, Africa, and wherever there are any missionaries from the Societies in England'.

Thus an immense number of praying persons are engaged at the same hour in their supplications to the God of all grace, on behalf of a world lying in the Wicked One, and for the spread of that glorious gospel which is the power of God to human salvation; and thus the plan of union, which good Mr Edwards so strongly recommended, is, in no inconsiderable degree, adopted in the Christian world. (George Burder's preface to an abridged copy of Edwards' *Humble Attempt* published by the L.M.S. in 1814 and translated into French in 1823.)

In 1792, three years after Sutcliff's republication of the *Humble Attempt*, William Carey (1761-1834) published his *Enquiry into the Obligations of Christians, to Use Means for the Conversion of the Heathens*, which clearly shows the influence both of Edwards' writings and of the Prayer Call which developed from it. He cites Edwards' *Humble Attempt* to refute the idea of 'some learned divines' that 'the time is not yet come that the heathen should be converted' because the two witnesses of Revelation 11 must be slain first and other Scriptures fulfilled. He also urges 'fervent and united prayer' as 'one of the first, and most important duties incumbent upon us' referring to Zechariah 12:10, one of the passages used by Edwards, and he expresses his belief in 'the prophecies concerning the increase of Christ's kingdom' and 'the glorious out-pouring of the Spirit, which we expect at last'. On 2 October of the same year, 'the Particular-Baptist Society for propagating the Gospel among the heathen' was born and in the following year Carey left for India as its first missionary, Andrew Fuller being the first secretary of the new society.

In the *Enquiry* Carey also appeals three times to the example of David Brainerd of whom he had read in Edwards' edition of his diaries. According to Ryland this volume became 'almost a second Bible to him'. He took a copy of it to India and often drew strength and encouragement from it. In this further way the literary output of Jonathan Edwards was a vital factor in the birth of Protestant missions.

Other Evangelicals were quick to follow. David Bogue, Edward Williams and other Evangelical Congregationalists, together with Evangelical Anglicans such as Thomas Haweis, were the founding members of the Missionary Society founded in London in 1795. Church of Scotland Evangelicals such as John Erskine, thwarted by the Moderates in the General Assembly in 1796, formed the Edinburgh and Glasgow Missionary Societies in 1798. In 1799 Anglican Evangelicals including John Newton and Joseph Milner formed what later became the Church Missionary Society. These were all men who had been profoundly influenced in their Evangelical Calvinism and in their missionary vision by Jonathan Edwards. Among the Methodists, Thomas Coke was thwarted at least twice by John Wesley himself in his plan to establish a Methodist missionary society, but eventually succeeded after Wesley's death. (See Introduction) Although, as an Arminian his theology was probably not directly influenced in the same way as the Calvinists we have been considering, he was nevertheless profoundly impressed by the example of David Brainerd of whom he had read in Edwards' edition of the *Diary*: 'His humility, his self-denial, his perseverance and his flaming zeal for God, are exemplary indeed.'

In Continental Europe as well as in North America, the same influence can be traced as the number of missionary societies multiplied (the Netherlands Missionary Society, 1797; the American Board of Commissioners for Foreign Mission, 1810; the American Baptist Missionary Union, 1814; the Basel Evangelical Missionary Society, 1815; the Missionary Society of the Methodist Episcopal Church, 1819; the Domestic and Foreign Missionary Society of the Protestant Episcopal Church of the USA, 1821; the Paris Society for Evangelical Missions, 1822.) And, as someone has said, the rest is history – the last two centuries of missionary activity which followed have resulted in the worldwide spread of the Christian Faith. The task is still unfinished but we can enter into it with the same confidence in the Gospel as the 'power of God for salvation' that our forbears did.

Charts

Comparative Time Chart

While it is not possible here to produce the kind of time-line found in *Christian History* magazine or in on-line Encyclopaedias, it is still useful to see a comparative time chart of the two hundred years or so when the characters mention in this book lived. Events in Europe, the British Isles and America which are often studied separately derive extra significance when they are seen against a wider backcloth.

Date	Europe	British Isles	America
1415	Jan Hus, early Czech reformer martyred		
1457	*Unitas Fratrum* formed by followers of Hus in Bohemia		
1517	Martin Luther nails his *95 Theses* to door of church in Wittenberg. Reformation begins		
1590	Saravia writes book on ministry and mission		
1592	*Comenius born in Eastern Moravia*		
1603		Elizabeth I dies. James VI of Scotland crowned in England as James I	
1604		King James I thwarts most Puritan reforms in their "Millenary Petition"	
1608		Puritan separatists from town of Scrooby migrate to Netherlands to avoid persecution	
1611		Authorised Version of Bible	
1618	Thirty Years War begins with revolt in Prague		
1620	Defeat of Protestant army in Battle of White Mountain near Prague
Comenius in hiding	Scrooby separatists return to England and set out for America --- ------------------>	"Pilgrim Fathers" set up Plymouth Colony at Cape Cod, Massachusetts
1625		James I dies. Charles I crowned	
1628	Comenius leaves for Leszno, Poland		
1629		"Great Migration" of English Puritans to Massachusetts Bay begins	"Great Migration" of English Puritans to Massachusetts Bay begins
1631			John Eliot arrives in New England
1633		William Laud Archbishop of Canterbury	
1641		Comenius visits England to set up college
Richard Baxter pastor in Kidderminster	
1642	Comenius leaves England, visits Sweden, moves to Elbing, Prussia	Outbreak of English Civil War.	
1644			Thomas Mayhew Jr begins preaching to the Indians on the island of Martha's Vineyard
1645		Baxter chaplain in Cromwell's New Model Army
William Laud executed	
1646			John Eliot begins missionary work among Indians in Massachusetts
1647		Baxter returns to Kidderminster	
1648	Comenius returns to Leszno
Treaty of Westphalia ends
Thirty Years War but no provision for *Unitas Fratrum*		

1649		Execution of King Charles I. Commonwealth set up under Cromwell as Lord Protector. Company for the Propagation of the Gospel in New England set up by Parliament	
1650	Comenius moves to Sarospatak in Hungary		Eliot increasingly concerned that the Indian Christians are too scattered
1651			Eliot sets up first "praying town" at Natick
1655-1656	Comenius returns to Leszno but forced to flee. Settles in Amsterdam		
1660		Restoration of monarchy Charles II crowned	
1661		Savoy Conference. Baxter's proposed alternative liturgy rejected	
1662		Baxter and 2000 other Puritan ministers forced out of churches following Act of Uniformity. Baxter lives privately in London	
1663	Justinian von Weltz writes tracts on mission		Cotton Mather born in Boston
1668	Justinian von Weltz dies in Surinam		
1669		Baxter imprisoned for a week	
1670	Comenius dies in Amsterdam		
1675-1676			King Philip's War devastates Eliot's Indian churches
1681		Baxter's wife dies	
1685		Charles II dies, James II crowned. Baxter tried by Judge Jeffreys and imprisoned for 21 months	Cotton Mather ordained as minister
1688-9		"Glorious Revolution" James II flees, William & Mary crowned	
1690			John Eliot dies aged 86
1691		Richard Baxter dies in London	
1692			Witchcraft trials at Salem
1699			Cotton Mather appointed as a Commissioner of Indian Affairs

1700	Zinzendorf born in Dresden		
1701		Thomas Bray organises SPG	
1702		Anne Queen of England (till 1714) Philip Doddridge born	Cotton Mather's *Magnalia Christi Americana* published (in London)
1703		John Wesley born in Epworth	Jonathan Edwards born in East Windsor, Conn
1705	Philip Jakob Spener (founder of Pietism) dies		
1706	First two Pietist missionaries leave Halle for India		
1707		Charles Wesley born in Epworth Isaac Watts' *Hymns & Spiritual Songs* published	
1709			Cotton Mather begins correspondence with Pietist A W Boehm in London
1710	Zinzendorf studies in Halle (centre of Pietism)		
1714		George I King (till 1727)	
1716	Zinzendorf studies in Wittenberg (centre of orthodox Lutheranism)		Jonathan Edwards studies at Yale
1717	Christian David's first visit to Sehlen in Moravia		Cotton Mather begins direct correspondence with Halle and Tranquebar
1720		John Wesley to Oxford	
1722	Moravians begin migration to Saxony. Herrnhut founded		Jonathan Edwards pastor in New York
1723		Robert Millar publishes *History of the Propagation of Christianity and Overthrow of Paganism*	Increase Mather (Cotton Mather's father) dies
1726			Jonathan Edwards to Northampton as assistant to Solomon Stoddard (his grandfather)
1727	Moravians renewed in powerful experience of Revival	John Wesley curate in Lincs George II King (till 1760)	Jonathan Edwards marries Sarah Pierrepont
1728			Cotton Mather dies
1729		John Wesley returns to Oxford and takes over leadership of the Holy Club	Solomon Stoddard dies JE sole pastor
1732	First two Moravian missionaries leave for West Indies		
1733	Three Moravian missionaries to Greenland		
1734	Moravian missionaries to Lapland and Georgia		Revival begins in Northampton and Connecticut Valley
1735	Moravian missionaries to Surinam	John and Charles Wesley leave as missionaries for Georgia George Whitefield converted	Revival in Northampton comes to end
1736	Moravian missionaries to Guinea Coast Zinzendorf banished from Saxony. Property leased in Wetteravia	George Whitefield starts preaching; revival begins Charles Wesley returns to England	Revivals in New Jersey under Tennents
1737	Moravian missionaries to South Africa Zinzendorf cosectrated as Moravian bishop	Revival grows through Whitefield's preaching. Doddridge first interest in Moravian's missionary activity	
1738	Moravian missionaries to Jews in Amsterdam. Building of Herrnhaag in Wetteravia	John Wesley returns to England Charles & John Wesley experience conversion/renewal	George Whitefield three months in Georgia Zinzendorf in West Indies

1739	Moravian missionaries to Algeria	George Whitefield & John Wesley begin open-air preaching	Zinzendorf returns from West Indies
1740	Moravian missionaries to North American Indians, Ceylon, Romania & Constantinople	George Whitefield sails for America. Doddridge begins correspondence with Zinzendorf	Whitefield in South then goes to New England Great Awakening begins. Whitefield visits Jonathan Edwards in Northampton
1741		Philip Doddridge makes proposals for missionary society	Zinzendorf in North America
1743	Beginning of "Sifting Period" (Lasted till 1750)		Zinzendorf leaves North America
1747		Thomas Coke born	David Brainerd dies in Edwards' home
1750			Jonathan Edwards leaves Northampton
1751		Philip Doddridge dies in Lisbon	Jonathan Edwards settles in Stockbridge
1752	Zinzendorf's son Christian Renatus dies at age 25	Zinzendorf in England	
1755		Zinzendorf leaves England	
1758			Jonathan Edwards moves to Princeton dies of smallpox
1760		George III King	
1761		William Carey born	
1771			Francis Asbury goes to America as Wesley's "General Assistant"
1775			American War of Independence begins
1776			American Declaration of Independence
1777		Thomas Coke joins Methodists	
1778		Coke's proposal to Methodist Conference for mission to Africa rejected	
1783			American War of Independence ends (Treaty of Paris)
1784		Coke proposes *A Plan of the Society for the Establishment of Missions among the Heathens* - rejected	Coke sent to America as "Superintendent" and to ordain Francis Asbury
1786		Coke publishes *Address to the Pious and Benevolent* proposing missionary support. Lukewarm support from Wesley & Conference	Coke visits West Indies with positive results
1789	French Revolution		
1791		John Wesley dies	
1792	August Gottlieb Spangenberg (Zinzendorf's successor) dies. French Revolutionary Wars (till 1799)	William Carey's *Enquiry*. Baptist Missionary Society formed	Methodist missionaries sent to West Indies
1793		William Carey leaves for India	
1795-- >		London Missionary Society and scores of others founded in UK, Europe & USA (see list in Conclusion)	
1813		Thomas Coke leaves for India but dies at sea on the way	
1814	Fall of Napoleon		

Further Reading: articles, books and websites

General

If your appetite has been whetted by reading about these servants of God in past times, you might be interested in following up on some of them. *The Lion History of Christianity* edited by Tim Dowley (Oxford: Lion Publishing, 1990) provides a good, general overview of the whole 2000 years of Christianity on a popular level. However, by far the best introduction to Christian history, and to a number of the men featured in this book, is the *Christian History* magazine published by Christianity Today in the United States but easily available in Britain from any Christian bookshop. The first issue published in 1982 featured Zinzendorf and the Moravians and a number of the subsequent ones have dealt with Christian leaders mentioned in this book. The format is easy to read, with pictures, maps and excellent time charts but at the same time everything is produced by scholars and experts on the particular subject. The first fifty issues are also available on a CD-ROM. Their website http:// www.christianitytoday.com/history/ is well worth a visit.

Other websites which cover the whole 2000 years of Church history include the Christian Classics Ethereal Library at http://www.ccel.org/ (which has also produced a CD-ROM of everything on the site), and the Hall of Church History, subtitled 'Theology from a Bunch of Dead Guys' (!) at http://www.gty.org/ ~ phil/hall.htm – well worth a look! For pictures of many figures in church history, including some we have dealt with in this book see http://solo4.abac.com/echoes/museum/index.htm.

See also Computer Assisted Theology: Internet Resources for the Study and Teaching of Theology at http://info.ox.ac.uk/ctitext/theology/#history which will give hyperlinks to many others.

The *Biographical Dictionary of Christian Missions* edited by Gerald H. Anderson (Grand Rapids & Cambridge, 1998), a comprehensive work of 840 pages, has brief but useful biographies of all those featured in this book. There are some very good, informative maps relevant to the 17th and 18th centuries in *The Atlas of the Bible and the History of Christianity* edited by Tim Dowley (BFBS 1997) pages113-127.

Introduction

The period from the Reformation till the beginnings of the modern Protestant missionary movement is covered briefly in an article by the author already mentioned in a footnote, R.E.Davies, 'The Great Commission from Calvin to Carey', Evangel 14:2 (Summer 1996) pp 44-49. If you would like to read Martin Luther's *Ninety Five Theses*, they are available online in a number of places; Project Wittenberg at http://www.iclnet.org/pub/resources/text/wittenberg/luther/web/ninetyfive.html, also http://www.gty.org/~phil/history/95theses.htm and http://www.fordham.edu/halsall/source/luther95.txt.

William Carey's *Enquiry* is available for reading or downloading at http://www.grace.org.uk/mission/enquiry0.html and http://www.baptistpage.com/Reading/Enquiry/carey_enquiry.html.

Some background information on **Adrian Saravia** is found at http://www.jesus-is-lord.com/transla3.htm. He was one of those who drafted the Belgic Confession (1561), later moved from the Netherlands to England and was sent by Queen Elizabeth I's Council as a sort of missionary to the islands of Guernsey and Jersey, where he was one of the first Protestant ministers. Back in England he had a number of positions, including Prebendary of Gloucester, of Canterbury (1595) and of Westminster (1601). He was a friend of Richard Hooker the author of the famous *Laws of Ecclesiastical Polity*, the definitive defence of Anglicanism, and was an advisor to Archbishop Whitgift. He was an acknowledged expert in the Biblical languages and was one of the translators of the Authorized Version (1611).

The best work on **Justinian van Weltz** in English is by a Lutheran missiologist James A. Scherer *Justinian Welz: Essays by an Early Prophet of Mission* (Eerdmans, 1966) which contains Justinian's tracts on mission together with an introduction. There are a large number of writings in German, including a well-documented article with excellent bibliography by Werner Raupp in *Bibliographisches Kirchenlexicon*, Verlag Traugot Bautz, Band XIII (1998) columns 737-742 available on the Web at http://www.bautz.de/bbkl/w/welz.shtml.

For **Robert Millar** see Ronald E. Davies, 'Robert Millar – an Eighteenth Century Scottish Latourette', *Evangelical Quarterly* 62:2 (1990) pages 143-156. There is also a good article on him in *Dictionary of Scottish Church History and Theology* edited by Nigel M. de S. Cameron & D. F. Wright, T & T Clark 1993.

There are no books currently in print on or by **Philip Doddridge**. There is an article on his life by A.C.Clifford, 'The Christian Mind of Philip Doddridge (1702-1751), in *Evangelical Quarterly* 56:4 (1984) pp 227-242, another on the Grace Online Library webpage at http://www.graceonlinelibrary.org/full.asp?ID-433 and a longer one on the Heath Chrisitan Bookshop site at http://www.christian-bookshop.co.uk/free/biogs/dodd1.htm . A number of websites feature works by Doddridge, including the complete text of one of his best-known works *The Rise and Progress of Religion in the Soul.* See in the Christian classics Ethereal Library mentioned above http://www.ccel.org/d/doddredge/rise/rise.htm.

The best study of **Thomas Coke** is J Vickers, *Thomas Coke: Apostle of Methodism* (London & Nashville 1969). See also J A Vickers, 'One-man Band: Thomas Coke and Origins of Methodist Missions', *Methodist History* 34 (1996) pp 135-147. There is a brief biographical note at http://www.victorshepherd.on.ca/Heritage/Coke.htm and an engraving of Coke together with a printed *Address to the Subscribers to the West Indian Mission* of 1788 at http://rylibweb.man.ac.uk/data1/dg/methodist/coke.html#coke2a

Chapter 1 Jan Amos Comenius: Education and Mission

The best introduction to Comenius is the issue of *Christian History* VI.1 which is devoted to his life and work. There is also a new biography, Daniel Murphy *Comenius*, Irish Academic Press (1995), and a number of English translations of his works are also becoming available. *The Labyrinth of the World and the Paradise of the Heart* was published by R. A. Kessinger Publishing Co in 1992 and a new translation by the Paulist Press in their series of *Classics of Western Spirituality* in 2000. His *Orbis Pictus* was published in 2000 by R A Kessinger Publishing Co who in 1992 gave us *The Great Didactic of Comenius* edited by M.W. Keatinge. Two volumes of his *Panorthosia or Universal Reform* are available from Sheffield Academic Press translated by A. M. O. Dobbie, who also translated his *Pampaedia* published by Regency Press (London & New York) in

1986. The name of Comenius is used by a number of language institutes and other schools in the Czech Republic and elsewhere. The European Union has a Comenius Project dedicated to European Co-operation on School Education (see http://europa.eu.int/comm/education/socrates/comenius). There is also a 75 minute film dramatization of *Comenius: Father of Modern Education* available from Gateway Films. The neglect of Comenius outside his home country seems to be coming to an end!

Chapter 2 Richard Baxter: Evangelism and Mission

Christian Focus Publications have an edition of Baxter's autobiography *Richard Baxter – Autobiography: The pastor's pastor* and Evangelical Press produce an abridgment of *The Reformed Pastor* under the title *The Ministry We Need* (1997). Crossway Books have an edition of his memoir of his wife's life and death with an introduction by J I Packer entitled *A Grief Sanctified: Passing Through Grief to Peace and Joy* (1998). Dr Packer, whose Oxford DPhil thesis was on Baxter, has also given a 'St Atholin's Lectureship Charity Lecture' which was published in 1991 with the title *A Man for All Ministries: Richard Baxter, 1615-1691.* The four massive volumes of Baxter's *Practical Works* are published by Soli Deo Gloria Publishers and Cambridge University Press has an edition of *The Holy Commonwealth* with an introduction by William Lamont (1994). A number of websites have online editions of his works, for example the Christian. Classics Ethereal Library at http://www.ccel.org/ has *The Saints' Everlasting Rest*. However, the best place to start is the Richard Baxter Home page at http://members.aol.com/augusteen/Baxter.html which has a vast number of links as well as many of his writings. See also the Richard Baxter Society at http://

www.members.tripod.com/ ~ oboofcom/index-3.html
which has more links!

Chapter 3 Cotton Mather: Ecumenism and Mission

One of the best books ever written on Mather is, sadly,
out of print. Richard Lovelace's *The American Pietism of
Cotton Mather: Origins of American Evangelicalism* Eerdmans
1979 originated as a Harvard ThD. It is an excellent
treatment of the many facets of the man and his work,
including his interest in world mission. As far as Mather's
writings are concerned, the Banner of Truth Trust publish
his major work *Magnalia Christi Americana* under the title
The Great Works of Christ in America in two volumes. The
Cotton Mather Home Page http://www.gty.org/ ~ phil/
mather.htm is still being developed but it already contains
some of his works and some useful links.

There is a website dedicated to the Salem Witchcraft
Trials which is unsympathetic towards Mather but it does
contain the text of his *Memorable Providences, Relating to
Witchcrafts and Possessions* (1689). It is found at http://
www.law.umkc.edu/faculty/projects/ftrials/salem/
SALEM.HTM.

Chapter 4 Jonathan Edwards: Eschatology and Mission

Jonathan Edwards is undoubtedly the best-known of
the characters we have dealt with in this book. Many of
his writings are available in print as well as on the Web,
especially his works on Revival and some of his sermons.
A few years ago at the height of interest in the 'Toronto
Blessing' Edwards was being quoted with approval by
supporters and opponents! His edition of David Brainerd's
Journal is arguably the best-known and most influential

missionary biography ever! It seems at present that in academic circles there is a whole 'Jonathan Edwards Industry' as books, articles and doctoral dissertations continue to be produced in large numbers. According to one bibliography of writings on Edwards, the number of dissertations etc, devoted to his thought has doubled every year since the 1950s as nearly every aspect of his thought is subjected to analysis.

The best general biography of Edwards which pays close attention to his thought in many practical areas, including Revival, Christian living and missions is Iain H. Murray, *Jonathan Edwards: A New Biography* Banner of Truth Trust 1987. The Banner of Truth also publishes a complete edition of his works (first produced in the nineteenth century) as well as selections. Since 1957 Yale University Press have been producing a definitive critical edition both of his published writings but also the vast number of his unpublished works which it hopes to finish in AD2003, the 300th anniversary of his birth! To date, eighteen volumes have appeared each costing around £50! There are also three home pages on the Internet devoted to his works, one of them devoted to the Yale edition http://www.yale.edu/wje/the second where it is possible to download many of his sermons and other writings http://jonathanedwards.com/ and the third giving links to related websites http://www.hillsdale.edu/dept/Phil%26Rel/JE/Links.html. A number of other websites have a selection of his works, including the Christian Classics Ethereal Library already mentioned. There is also a CD-ROM available which contains the complete Banner of Truth edition of his works, Iain Murray's biography, John Gerstner's three volume *The Rational Biblical Theology of Jonathan Edwards* and some notes on Scripture and a commentary on Hebrews which is not included in the 'complete' edition (information is on the last-mentioned website).

On Edwards' own missionary interest and involvement see Ronald E. Davies, 'Jonathan Edwards: Missionary Biographer, Theologian, Strategist, Administrator, Advocate – and Missionary', *International Bulletin of Missionary Research* 21.2 (April 1997) pages 60-67, and on his profound influence on the Protestant missionary movement a generation after his death see R.E.Davies, 'Jonathan Edwards, theologian of the missionary awakening', *Evangel* 17.1 (Spring 1999) EMA Occasional Paper No 3.

Chapter 5 Count Zinzendorf: Engagement and Mission

As mentioned at the beginning of this chapter, the *Christian History* journal began its publication in 1982 with an issue devoted to Zinzendorf and the Moravians who 250 years before had sent their first missionaries to the island of St Thomas in the West Indies. One of the best accounts of Zinzendorf's involvement in mission is A. J. Lewis, *Zinzendorf the Ecumenical Pioneer: A Study in the Moravian Contribution to Christian Mission and Unity*. It was published by SCM in 1962 but has been reprinted more recently, although it seems to be unavailable at present. Two books on Zinzendorf which are in print are Arthur J. Freeman, *An Ecumenical Theology of the Heart: The Theology of Count Nikolaus von Zinzendorf*, the Moravian Church in America 1998 and a reprint of John Weinlick, *Count Zinzendorf: the Story of his Life and Leadership in the Renewed Moravian Church* 1956. Both of these are obtainable from the excellent website which has been produced to celebrate

the 300th anniversary of Zinzendorf's birth in 1700 http:/
/www.zinzendorf.com. This site has many fascinating
documents, articles and pictures. Three videos have been
produced and are obtainable from the site, one *The First
Fruits*, made in 1982 and two only recently completed.
There are a large number of links which are worth
following up and you can read and download a complete
copy of J.E.Hutton's *History of the Moravian Church*. and
also one of Zinzendorf's sermons. You can also buy
Zinzendorf coffee mugs and other 'collectibles'!

There is a discussion of some of Zinzendorf's more
controversial ideas and expressions in Gary S. Kinkel *Our
Dear Mother the Spirit: An Investigation of Count Zinzendorf's
Theology and Praxis* University Press of America 1990.

Conclusion

In addition to the article quoted, there are two books which
give useful background information: Timothy George,
Faithful Witness: The Life and Mission of William Carey, IVP:
1991. (This had Carey's Enquiry in full in an Appendix)
and Michael A. G. Haykin, One Heart and One Soul: John
Sutcliff of Olney, his friends and his times, Evangelical
Press, 1994.

Hopefully you will find these further references and
links helpful in building up a fuller picture of the lives and
ideas of these servants of God of former years.

Further books from
Christian Focus

Mission to the Headhunters

How God's Forgiveness
Transformed Tribal Enemies
Frank and Marie Drown

'...an incredible story of how God used this mid-west American
couple who had simply responded to His call. As a result, an
unreached people has been transformed for His glory.'

Dr. Jean Barsness,
Missions Consultant and Educator

'The book is straightforward and beautifully written. It's a page-
turner. I was staggered and rebuked, helped and cheered by the
steadfast faithfulness of this humble (I'm sure they would say
merely ordinary) couple. Read it!'

Elisabeth Elliot,
Author of "Through Gates of Splendor"

'What an incredible story of the Lord building His church...
Don't miss reading about this challenge of the century!'

Dr Carl McMindes,
President, Gospel Missionary Union,
Kansas City, Missouri

Frank and Marie were missionaries in Ecuador for thirty-seven
years. During that time they saw huge changes as they reached the
Indians with the Gospel. This is their remarkable story.

ISBN 1 85792 721 4

A STORY OF SUFFERING
MARTHA LE AZUMA

FIRE
IN MY
BONES

DICK ANDERSON

Fire in My Bones
The Story of Pioneering Mission in Africa
Dick Anderson

Dick Anderson and his wife Joan were pioneering missionaries in Turkana, Kenya, spending many years in the front line of world evangelisation. Their ground-breaking experiences were used by Africa Inland Mission (AIM) to evaluate the possibility of mission the length and breadth of Africa. This is not just another story of missionary success, Dick critically reviews his work at the mission in Turkana, and evaluates how the mission has progressed since they it began in the late fifties.

'...testimony of one of those in whose heart has burned the passion of Paul for those as yet denied access to the message of the gospel. If this book kindles such a fire in the bones of some of the Lord's people - it will have served its purpose well.' **John Brand, Africa Inland Mission**

No one reading this biography will remain unchallenged...thrilling and gripping account of risks undertaken and dangers faced for the sake of the Gospel.' **Timothy G Alford**

'His insights on the cost of leadership are worth the price of the book alone. However there is much more to learn about the value and diversity of partnership and godly principles for mission in today's world.'
Stanley Davies, Executive Director, Global Connections

'The Andersons have a remarkable story to tell covering quite the most exciting and challenging period of Africa's encounter with the Gospel.'
Patrick Johnstone, WEC, Author of *Operation World*

ISBN 1 85792 676 5

Global Warning
Third Millennium threats to Jesus'
great commission mandate
Norman Mackay

'...*a soul-stirring wake up call for Christians living in a self-absorbed age. It will rekindle your heart with a passion for world evangelisation.*'
John F. MacArthur, Grace Community Church, Sun Valley California

'*If God is to stir the slumbering embers of Christian hearts in the West our passion for missions must be rekindled. Norman Mackay's straightforward, easy to read, and quite convincing work might well be used to awaken many to the real issues.*'
John H. Armstrong, President, Reformation & Revival Ministries

'*Mission is the raison-d'etre of the Christian Church. Yet Christians can easily find a thousand different reasons for avoiding it. This book is an uncompromising critique of such evasiveness and should disturb every evangelical conscience. It should also fire us all to go and tell every man and woman, "I have good news for you."*'
Donald Macleod, Principal, Free Church of Scotland College

'*This unique cutting-edge missions book will not be easy for some of us to digest, but the message is greatly needed at this moment in history.*'
George Verwer, International Director, Operation Mobilisation.

Rev. Norman Mackay and his wife, Alison, served with WEC International for several years as pioneer missionaries in the Central Asian Republics of the former USSR.

ISBN 1 85792 6595